From Big Predicaments *to* Big Possibilities!

12 Kingdom Principles for Personal Financial Gain

by

Ferron Fitzroy Francis, D. Min.

From Big Predicaments to Big Responsibilities
published by Watersprings Publishing,
a division of Watersprings Media House, LLC.
P.O. Box 1284 Olive Branch, MS 38654
www.waterspringsmedia.com

Contact publisher for bulk orders and permission requests.

Copyright © 2022 Ferron Fitzroy Francis, D.Min. All rights reserved.

No part of this publication may be reproduced, distributed, or transmitted in any form or by any means, including photocopying, recording, or other electronic or mechanical methods, without the prior written permission of the publisher, except in the case of brief quotations embodied in critical reviews and certain other noncommercial uses permitted by copyright law.

Printed in the United States of America.

Photograph by JeNean Lendor

ISBN-13: 978-1-948877-99-2

Contents

CHAPTER 1: THE BIG PREDICAMENT!
How Do We Get Out of This Situation?. 1

CHAPTER 2: THE BIG DEAL
Am I a Giver or a Trader? 19

CHAPTER 3: THE BIG DIFFERENCE
Secret of a Successful Steward 33

CHAPTER 4: THE BIG DISCOVERY
Untapped Resources. 51

CHAPTER 5: THE BIG BREAKTHROUGH
Stop Struggling...Enjoy Living. 61

CHAPTER 6: THE BIG REWARD
What Does Our Giving Say About Our Relationship with God? 73

CHAPTER 7: THE BIG PROBLEM
A Deafening Silence from Many Pulpits on True Biblical Financial Stewardship 95

CHAPTER 8: THE BIG TRUTH
Our Churches Need Our Offerings 113

CHAPTER 9: THE BIG RESPONSIBILITY
Sharing the Reality That Stewardship
Is Not Optional. 139

CHAPTER 10: THE BIG BLESSING
What Does Stewardship Have to Do
with Salvation?. 159

CHAPTER 11: THE BIG PICTURE
What Does This Really Mean in
the Grand Scheme of Things?. 167

CHAPTER 12: THE BIG POSSIBILITIES
Enjoying Freedom in the Midst of Restriction 179

CHAPTER 13: THE BIG STORIES
Testimonies of the Transforming Power of God. 193

BIBLIOGRAPHY 221

ABOUT THE AUTHOR 223

Acknowledgments

I am deeply indebted to a large number of people who have inspired the writing of this book. I have been privileged to work with some of the most committed leaders in the Northeastern Conference of Seventh-day Adventists in stewardship ministry. I have learned so much from them; their contribution to this volume is saturated all throughout the pages.

To all of my colleagues in pastoral ministry who have encouraged and affirmed me as I ministered all over the Northeastern territory and beyond, I thank you for partnering with me. I would also like to thank God for Eslyn Phillip-Carter, the administrative assistant whom He has blessed me to work with. Thanks, Eslyn, for your support, creativity and commitment to the Stewardship ministry.

I would also like to thank Duwayne Rowe for his artwork, creativity and design of the covers of this book. I am so grateful to the reviewers Kaysian Gordon and Tracy John, who were so kind and generous in their task.. Special thanks to the publishers of this volume for the excellent work that they have done in making this volume available to all who are desiring a better understanding of what it means to be a good steward of God. I appreciate the counsel and suggestions made to present the message of this book in the most meaningful way.

A special debt of gratitude to my dear wife, Tosha-Lyn, and our two children, Andrew and Ashley-Ann. Thanks, family, for your love, support, patience, suggestions and confidence in me throughout the entire journey of this volume. Your contribution to the completion of this book is invaluable.

Most of all, I give God thanks and praise for His enlightenment, wisdom, and tremendous blessings that made this all possible.

Introduction

Money! That's what usually comes to mind first when we hear the word stewardship. Money management is an important aspect of stewardship. I believe that much time and energy needs to be invested in helping everyone to achieve some level of mastery regarding money management. However, if we narrow our view of stewardship to primarily money management, we will be addressing one of the symptoms of a problem and not the root cause. While I do believe that our management of money is one of the many things entrusted to us by God for which we ought to be good stewards, it is certainly not the most important thing. God has given to us so much more than money. Our lives are the most precious gifts God has entrusted unto us. Our first responsibility is to acknowledge and appreciate the gift of life before the things that add meaning and value to life.

At the heart of the presentation of the gospel is the message of stewardship. This of course is about managing life. For us to be great managers of the monies God has entrusted unto us, we first must learn how to be good managers of the life He has given us. That is, the life given at birth and eternal life given to all those who accept Jesus Christ as Lord and Savior of their lives.

The definition of stewardship that I like the most is: "Managing God's resources, God's way, for God's glory!" This comprehensive definition speaks of God as the central focus of stewardship. God owns everything. God is the giver of all good gifts. God allows us to become good managers of what He entrusts in our care. However, for us to manage God's resources in a manner that pleases Him, we first must have an intimate relationship with Him that would motivate us to manage the things He has entrusted unto us.

The more intimate, respectful and trusting the relationship is with God (the owner of everything) that I have, the more thoughtful and caring a steward I am likely to be of the things He has entrusted to me. Herein is the basic premise of this book: God's primary desire is our hearts and not the monies He has given to us. I believe that if God has our hearts completely, He will also help us manage the things He has given to us.

As stewards our greatest challenge is not the amount of money we have. While it is true for many of us that we would greatly appreciate having more money than we currently have, how we manage money of any sum large or small is most important. Even the quality of life that we lead is not based entirely upon what our bank accounts look like, but on the management we employ to govern the monies entrusted to us. Our greatest challenge, therefore, is how we manage our money based on the relationship we have with God. What we do with all our money we have is an indicator of the nature of our relationship with God. The purpose of this book is to challenge the reader to examine her/his relationship with God as the determining factor that governs our stewardship of life. It is my hope that as each reader goes from one page to the next, it will become crystal clear that everyone can receive maximum benefits from the monies entrusted to each person regardless of the amount in their possession. Our need for money might not be as great as our need to manage money using Christian principles.

One of the basic needs of any person or organization, including the church, is financial stability. That is, the ability to successfully address our financial obligations and the ability to save. The church's success as an organization depends largely on the stewardship of the money it has been entrusted with. With money being of such great importance, the church must invest a considerable amount of money to ensure that its financial affairs are managed by some of the most skilled and talented individuals. Every person in the church, beginning with its leadership [pastors], is responsible for demonstrating obedience and honesty to the divine mandate of being a good steward. William Barclay argued that a person's character, honesty or dishonesty, straightness or crookedness "can be seen, and nowhere better, than in...daily business dealings. The life a [person] lives is in its own way a preparation for eternal life."[1] A person's management of the monies entrusted to her or him is a reflection on the relationship that exists between themselves and the divine.

My intention in this brief volume is to suggest some practical and spiritual principles that if employed by God-fearing individuals, groups or organizations will result in people experiencing what I believe is God's ideal for us, to stop struggling and enjoy living until the end of the world as we experience it currently. I offer these principles to foster meaningful

---

1   William Barclay, Ethics in a Permissive Society (New York: Harper and Row, 1971), p. 162.

dialogue among church leadership at all levels and members who desire to become good stewards of God. It is my hope that this work will serve as a new horizon for many to look at their responsibility as Christian stewards and the church's responsibility to God as a community of Believers. At the end of this volume I desire that everyone who took the time to read this book will conclude that Christian stewardship is not an optional quality or characteristic that some Christians should possess, but rather a natural part of the Christian life of every sincere Christian who has an intimate relationship with God. So as you navigate your way through the pages of this book, my greatest hope is not to engender guilt or to massage self-righteousness, or to espouse any particular religious sentiments or ideologies, but rather to highlight truth from the biblical blueprint as a guide in helping us to gain mastery over selfishness and strength in generosity.

Let me also express sincere gratitude and appreciation to the editors of this book and the Northeastern Conference of Seventh-day Adventists constituency for allowing me the opportunity to serve as the Stewardship Ministry Director since 2016. Each chapter in this book concludes with an all-important question from the chapter that lends itself to a summary of the chapter in the answer given. This is followed by a "Think about this question" that causes the reader to reflect on her or his responsibility to the main message of the chapter.

I thank God for my family, colleagues and church family who have poured so much wisdom, knowledge and copious blessings into my life. This book would not have been the same without your invaluable contribution. Again, I say thank you!

Preface

More Questions than Answers

This is a book that I was inspired to write. I have often heard about writers and aspiring writers who say they have a book churning on the inside that they are burning with passion and desire to write. I have had a passion for stewardship for several years and have not found a book that addresses the subject from a more comprehensive approach. Therefore, I decided to create what I wanted to see.

Several years ago, I was wrestling with what it really means to be a good steward. I thought that if I got to a place where I was returning my tithe and offering consistently, then I would gain mastery over this matter of stewardship. This would result in me receiving the blessing of Malachi 3:10, which says, "...the Lord of host will open the windows of heaven and pour you out a blessing, that there shall not be room enough to receive it." This was my motivation to gain mastery over tithe and offering, so that I could live large and in charge of an abundance of financial blessings. I soon learned that stewardship is far more than returning tithe and offering.

As I delved deeper into what stewardship is really all about, I discovered that this was an all-encompassing management of life affair. I was blown away by what it really meant to be a good steward—managing life in a manner that pleases God. I was excited and overwhelmed at the same time. I had more questions than answers; why was I led to believe that stewardship was just about returning tithe and offering? When would I be told that there are strong connections between how I manage the other areas of my life and my finances? Why wasn't I told that God is not only interested in me returning tithe and offering, but that he is concerned about all the monies I am blessed with to use for other purposes? Why was I led to believe that returning tithe and offering was based on whether I can afford to? The questions kept flooding my mind; never before I was so strongly impacted by the subject of stewardship. Never was I more redirected than I was by being reintroduced to stewardship like I never saw before. The message of stewardship was so transformative, so revolutionary, so life-changing, so unlike what I had been taught, I knew I had to share it with as many people as possible.

However, for one reason or another I kept delaying the start of this manuscript. Even when I began writing, I took extended breaks that had nothing to do with writer's block or fatigue. There was just no justifiable reason for the delay most times. In hindsight, the delays turned out to be blessings I had no idea would come my way. As I shared my journey with my family, I got feedback and insights that were second to none. Even the title of the book and some of the chapters resulted from the input I received from them, especially my daughter Ashley-Ann.

One of the things I thought about for several years that seemed to be a major disconnection between practice and reality is the importance that many churches and higher church organizations gave to stewardship. Even from a limited view of stewardship being understood as prompting the giving of money, the importance of the stewardship leader was very limiting even though money was so important to the church or the higher church organization. Stewardship might be one of the most misunderstood, yet beneficial spiritual disciplines in our churches and church organizations. Since the role of money is so important in funding these churches and organizations, it would be assumed that church leadership at any level would be providing all the resources and support necessary to the stewardship personnel to achieve the best return. Mistakenly, this is seldom the case. Stewardship is often relegated to an almost obscure reality in many churches and higher organizations.

I believe that for a very long time we have been looking at stewardship "through a glass darkly" (1 Corinthians 13:12). We have looked at stewardship primarily as our obligation to God in tithe and to a lesser extent our offerings as well. As a result, we have been denying ourselves the many blessings God has in store for us if we broaden our lens and look at stewardship through the vast telescope that God would have us use to see the copious blessings He has in store for us. I remember the day I had an epiphany about stewardship and our relationship with God. It was transformative because I could see clearly that my management of the resources entrusted to me would be managed based on my relationship with the owner of the things I am asked to take care of. My relationship with God was the basis for my attitude and gratitude as a steward of His blessings. Maybe I was not in love with God as much as I thought, if my management of the resources He entrusted unto me did not demonstrate the same love for the things that belong to Him.

This book deals with some of the fundamentals and practical principles of what it means to be a good steward. I am writing from the knowledge and experience I have gained as a local church leader, auditor, pastor and Stewardship Ministry Director for the over sixty thousand members that make up the Northeastern Conference of Seventh-day Adventists. I hope that this book will provide you with spiritual and practical answers to the question of what it means to be a good Christian steward.

CHAPTER 1

The Big Predicament!

How Do We Get Out of This Situation?

Sometimes it seems like we really don't have to look too far or go anywhere to find ourselves in serious problems. Even harder to deal with is when our problems turn for the worse and become a predicament. I heard once that the difference between a problem and a predicament is that problems will eventually have solutions, while predicaments have outcomes. When we find ourselves in a predicament, our backs are against the wall and we have no idea what the outcome will be.

Sometimes we find ourselves in predicaments that we are responsible for. We made poor choices and have to nervously wait to see the outcome. However, there are times when we find ourselves in predicaments that we absolutely had no hand in. We currently find ourselves in a global pandemic predicament that is ravishing the world. Thousands are dying every day and ten thousands are being hospitalized. This predicament and its gut-wrenching effects do not seem to be going away any time soon. Despite the best efforts from the scientific and medical communities we are struggling with the outcome of this massive devastation every day. What will the outcome look like when this is behind for good? No one really knows the answer to this most important question. Living with such great uncertainty has caused many anxiety, fear, and distress. The effects of this tragic occurrence on the world since 2019 has created so much social, political, psychological, emotional, financial and spiritual unrest for almost all people on the planet. For many people, we were already dealing with several different predicaments before the discovery of the coronavirus, so the coronavirus pandemic has only added one more predicament to our list of difficulties and despairing situations that we must try to navigate successfully. Racism and financial difficulties are only two of the many predicaments many people have been dealing with for the last several decades.

Since the coronavirus pandemic surfaced on the shores worldwide from late 2019 to early 2020, many people have concluded that this is the most devastating predicament the world has ever seen in recent history. While I agree that this predicament may be the worst thing I have experienced in the last two or three decades, I am cognizant that the deadliest predicament the world has ever seen happened over six thousand years ago in the garden of Eden. What am I talking about? Yes, you are correct, I am speaking about when sin infected humanity. This pandemic predicament of sin that we are in has proven to be the worst thing that has ever affected the human race. We are bombarded with crime, violence, abuse and hatred that seems to be spinning out of control for thousands of years and counting. This predicament has been going on for so long that many people have resolved that the earth and all its inhabitants are doomed.

Stewardship Amid a Global Predicament

The mantra that most people have when going through difficulties usually sounds like this:

> *"Every man for himself!"*
> *"Only the strong survive!"*
> *"Do what's best for you!"*
> *"Take care of yourself first!"*
> *"Make sure you get what's yours!"*
> *"I've got to get mine!"*

And the list goes on and on, with the theme of selfishness as the underlying motive for our desires and actions. While some may say in a predicament it is natural for people to look out for themselves first, I must caution that it is the same sentiment of looking out for ourselves first that causes us to be in the predicament of sin. Adam and Eve put themselves first over God and His words and the result has been devastating since that moment. Therefore, we cannot keep on doing the same thing that got us in the predicament we are in and expect to have a better outcome.

The principle of stewardship was God's first assignment for humanity to be engaged in the garden of Eden even before sin. After sin, the principle of stewardship is still the number one thing God desires for us to master. Mastering stewardship during the predicament of sin is God's ideal for us. It is overcoming the power of sin through total reliance upon God. Despite the predicament of sin, God does not treat us as we deserve to be treated. He continues to give us far more than we could ever imagine or ask for. God gives to us to prepare us for a positive outcome when the predicament of sin is over.

God's purpose for calling us to be good stewards is to reinstate His relationship with humanity before sin. Therefore, our focus as good stewards is to do those things that will enhance our relationships with God. As you read this book and desire to become a good steward to receive copious measures of financial and other material blessings from God, I need to let you know that your desires will only be satisfied if you make God your primary and greatest and greatest desire and not wealth and money. The material blessings God gives to us when we put Him first in our lives are as a result of His grace and mercy toward us. We never deserve the tremendous material blessings we receive, yet we should always be grateful for what we have been given.

During a predicament we are sometimes pushed to the limit. We are oftentimes physically and emotionally exhausted. One of the comforting realities as we go through a predicament from day to day is knowing that God still cares for us. Why is that comforting, you may ask, if God does not take us out of the predicament?

I believe the current coronavirus pandemic's financial impact on the world's economy will total in the trillions of dollars before we have a reprieve. The tragedies of our current predicament will be many. The death toll is already a staggering four million-plus people as of September 2021.[2] The death toll is climbing higher and higher every day. While we are suffering and struggling in this pandemic predicament, God is still asking us to be good stewards of all of life's resources. If there was ever a time when we could be *"eligible"* to receive a

---

2 https://www.worldometers.info/coronavirus/coronavirus-death-toll/

reprieve from being good stewards it should be during a pandemic predicament. Yet, there is no such reprieve by God. God still requires of us to be good stewards because even though our situations may have changed drastically, our God has not changed! Since God has not changed, despite the severity of the predicament we find ourselves in, we have great hope of navigating and remaining faithful to God as good stewards even though we may have no idea when our situation may change positively.

One of the most common predicaments most people find themselves in is a financial one. This is because people often make decisions about money based not only on the amount they have, but also on the amount they wish they had. The acquisition of several credit cards to purchase things when we do not have the money to pay off the credit card bill in a timely manner is one clear example of people making a decision on money based not on what they have, but what they wish they had. Since they are making decisions on what they wish they had, their financial reality is not always able to meet the demand of their wish list, resulting in a predicament that is not easily resolved. Being in a financial predicament and being told to return tithe and offering to God when a person receives income that cannot even meet their debt payments is very difficult for many people to honor. Logically this is not a choice most people make consistently when they are indebted to someone. So, since we realize that honoring God in a financial predicament is not going to be a logical decision, we are left to figure out how such a person will be able to make an illogical decision and believe that what he or she is doing is the correct thing that will result in them being free from the predicament they are in.

Since it is also sometimes illogical decision making that causes one to be in a financial predicament, it might not be too far-fetched for me to suggest that it will also take illogical decision making to get out of the predicament. Before you close the book and proclaim emphatically that this does not make sense, read the next few sentences and follow where I am going with this. I am suggesting that we take the illogical step of faith to climb out of the predicament that we are in. When we are asked to give at a time when we have great needs as well, it sounds crazy! However, we can give in these times because our giving is based on our faith in God, who supplies us with all we have. We believe God can and will supply all our needs. To believe that doing the opposite of conventional wisdom and thinking will provide you with the results you seek is not something that many economists and financial counselors will advise you to do.

There is absolutely nothing conventional, rational or logical about faith. Faith is not intrinsically able to get us our desired outcomes. Faith only becomes useful based on the person or object it is placed in. Faith in God in the midst of a predicament is not a plea of desperation because everything else has failed us. It is believing that God is sovereign, omnipotent, omniscient and omnipresent. It is believing in God as the supreme creator and owner of the world and everything in it Psalms 24:1. So, as we recognize the predicaments we are in, I believe it is more important for us to focus on how we can get out, rather than how we got there in the first place. This does not mean we should not take responsibility for our actions or be careful about the decisions others make that may impact our lives. The point here is that we do not spend too much time blaming ourselves or others, but rather on what it will take to get us out. This means that our primary focus is to get out of the predicament so we can be in a place where we can live the way God intends for us to live.

From Predicaments to Possibilities

We have already established that most people are in debt and do not have enough income to satisfy or eliminate at once. Still many more people are struggling to meet their monthly obligations to satisfy that small portion they have agreed to pay. For us to move from financial predicaments to financial possibilities, there are certain principles we must be willing to acknowledge, explore and apply to our financial situations. Before we examine some of these salient principles, let us look closely at the framework of what it means to acknowledge, explore and apply to our financial situations.

Before we examine what some of these salient principles are, let us look closely at the framework of what it means to acknowledge, explore and apply to our financial situations.

Acknowledge:

One of the most important things I have learned over the years I have been engaged in pastoral ministry is acknowledging when I am wrong and when I am in trouble. Psalms 46:1 (KJV) reminds me, "God is my refuge and strength and a very present help in trouble." Isaiah 43:2 (KJV) echoes similar sentiments by saying that "when thou pass through the waters, I will be with thee; and through the rivers they shall not overflow thee; when thou walks through the fire, thou shalt not be burned; neither shall the flame kindle upon thee." These two Bible verses remind me that my response to trouble and predicament should not be one of denial but acknowledgment for me to receive the help I need. When someone is drowning, a desperate attempt of screaming and waving of the arms to get the attention of others is the natural response for the person who would like to be rescued. Not acknowledging your predicament and trying to seek help will reduce the likelihood of one being rescued from it. I read a story once about a preacher and an atheistic barber that I believe captures the idea of what we ought to do when we find ourselves in a predicament:

> A preacher and an atheistic barber were walking through the city slums one day. The barber said to the preacher, "If there is a loving God, how can he allow poverty, war and suffering?"
>
> Just at that moment a disheveled man crossed the street. The pastor said, "You are a barber and claim to be a good one. How can you allow that man to go unkempt and unshaven?"
>
> "He never gave me a chance!" the barber replied.
>
> To which the pastor said, "Exactly. Men are what they are because they do not acknowledge God for the help they need!"[3]
>
> Acknowledging one's predicament and reaching out for the help necessary to remedy the situation is the first thing that will move a person from predicament to possibility.

---

[3] https://www.sermonillustrator.org/illustrator/sermon1a/preacher.htm

Explore:

Knowing that you are in a predicament is important. However, if knowledge of your predicament does not lead to explorations of ways and means of getting out of it as soon as possible, then knowing would not be beneficial. Exploration suggests seeking as many ways as possible to get to the best result, as opposed to depending on one way only. This does not mean we need to explore several sources, but rather several ways from any chosen source.

For many God-fearing individuals, God is the source to which they turn when they are in a predicament. God is not limited to provide us with the outcome we are hoping for by using the same resources He used before. Sometimes we miss out on our blessings because we are looking for God to show up the same way He showed up before, when He may be doing something new.

Therefore, we must not only seek God when we are in a predicament but also explore the possibility that God may not provide the outcome the same way for everyone in every situation. Isaiah 43:19 says, "Behold, I will do a new thing, now it shall spring forth; shall ye not know it? I will even make a way in the wilderness, and rivers in the desert."

Apply:

Acknowledging and exploring are only beneficial if the person in the predicament is willing to apply the principles recommended. If a person is unwilling to apply or do what is suggested and/or required, the desired outcome will never be achieved.

Applying sometimes can be challenging, difficult and remarkably strenuous to undertake. However, it is critically important that there is an established commitment to applying all that is necessary to obtain the necessary outcome.

Principles that will move you from predicament to possibility:

1. **Prayer** – Yes, prayer, is one of the most important spiritual resources we have when in a predicament. Prayer does not always have to have a formal structure or even be audible. What is most important is that we use this tremendous resource to intercede for God's intervention on our behalf or the behalf of others. The Bible is replete with examples of people in predicaments who utilized prayer and saw God provide them with desired results. Moses and the Israelites were standing before the Red Sea, with mountains on either side and Pharaoh's army behind them. However, when Moses called on God for help, God provided dry ground for him and the Israelites to cross over (Exodus 14).

    Daniel was cast in a lion's den, but God intervened on his behalf when he prayed and he was not harmed (Daniel 6). Prayer should not only be used because we are scared or in a predicament, but because we are confident that God can deliver us from any situation.

    The principle of prayer can and should be used in any predicaments. If you are reading this book and are in a financial predicament, please note that God specializes in situations like yours. The Bible gives the example of two widows who were experiencing financial predicaments. One lady had recently lost her husband in death and the creditors were on their way to collect debts he left behind. The widow had no money to repay her dead husband's debts, so the creditors decided that they would take and enslave her two sons to satisfy the debts. When she called on the Lord in prayer and went to seek counsel from the prophet Elijah, God intervened on her behalf by multiplying the little oil she had so she could sell it and obtain enough money to satisfy the debts and take care of her family (2 Kings 4). This took great faith on her part as she went to her neighbors collecting empty jars. We too must have faith that God can help us in our times of need. God also multiplied the last cruse jar of oil and morsel meal that the widow of Zarephath had to eat so she and her son did not die from starvation, but lived for many days. Whatever your financial predicament may look like, God is able to provide for your needs.

I remember going off to college with three suitcases, a duffel bag and $60 in my pocket to begin school. At the time, the school cost was $6,000 for room and board and tuition for 12 credits for the semester. I did not know how God would pay $6,000 from $60, but I prayed and asked God to intervene on my behalf. When I got to the dormitory and unloaded my luggage in the lobby, a gentleman came over to me and introduced himself as the dean. He informed me that I needed to be financially cleared before I could get a room in the dormitory. He directed me to the office where I should go and as I walked away from him, he called me back and asked me if I would like to work for him. With gleeful excitement I responded that I would be delighted. He said to me that I could work as a resident assistant dean and that I would be able to receive free room and board every semester. I hugged him and thanked the Lord for providing me with a place to live. God was not through answering my prayer; I went to the bursar's office and told the bursar that my housing predicament would be satisfied as I was a new employee of the dormitory. He handed me a bill of $4,000+ and told me I would still need to pay 70% of it to begin classes three days later on Monday morning. I took the bill to my room and continued praying. I got up Monday morning, dressed and went to classes for the day. I did the same thing the following morning and every morning for the rest of the first week of school. I continued going to classes every day, week and month for the semester, without any interruption or notices from the bursar's office. At the end of the semester, I was called to the bursar's office, where I was told I was the recipient of two academic scholarships that satisfied half of my tuition for the semester and that I was eligible to receive a loan to satisfy the other half. I praised God for His blessings and thanked Him for answering my prayer in the midst of my financial predicament.

2. **Faith** – Praying without faith that God can do the things we ask Him for is pointless. The Bible reminds us that if we do not have faith in God, then all that we do will not be pleasing to Him (Hebrews 11:6). We are also told that for us to have faith, we must read, hear and do what the Bible admonishes us to do (Romans 10:17).

   Being in a predicament can be an overwhelming and depressing experience. While we should continue to read the Bible during predicaments if possible, it is even more important to read, hear and practice what the Bible teaches before we are in a predicament.

However, it is still possible for us to develop genuine faith in a predicament as we hear from the word of God. Having faith in God in a predicament may result in God asking us to do things that are not rational or logical. Faith in God means that we believe God is more powerful than any situation we find ourselves in. Therefore, predicaments serve to reveal just how awesome a deliverer God is.

Several years ago, I was asked to serve as the pastor of a small church in New York State that had over 170 members on record, but only approximately 25 regular attendants. I soon discovered that the more accurate membership of the church was closer to 70 and not 170. The church had over $200,000 in debt and $5,000 in a building fund account, which represented its total financial position. The church did not have a portable or installed baptismal pool and I thought it was representative of the decline the church had experienced over the past 22 years. I decided that acquiring a baptismal pool would be my first priority. The members told me they did not know how I would get this done without adding to the already high debt they could not afford to liquidate. I began praying and trusting God to intervene on our behalf. After one year as the pastor of this small church, we purchased and installed a brand-new fiberglass pool. In addition, we were able to see God cancel away the entire financial debt we had, renovated the inside and outside of the church building and installed a brand-new electrical sign.

Faith in God is one of the key principles we need to live by when we are in a predicament. We will see and experience God doing the seemingly impossible for us when we exercise faith in Him. Faith is not wishing that God will act on our behalf, but rather truly believing that God can do all things! Faith in God in the midst of a predicament will help move us forward to endless possibilities.

3. **Courage** – is having mental strength to continue to do what is in one's best interest despite the difficulty and challenge you are faced with. That means that in the midst of a predicament, a person is willing to make choices as difficult as they may be to tackle suffering, pain and uncertainty. Courage causes us to attempt to do things we never thought we would be willing to do and confront things we never thought we would dare take on.

We become courageous amid adversity and predicament by acknowledging our weakness and vulnerability as we embrace the strength and power of God. This means that I recognize my limitations, but I do not settle in a pool of despair; instead, it motivates me to depend totally on God. I am willing to take the next step into the unknown and uncertainty because I believe God will help me to move forward even though it's extremely challenging and even fearful. Courage gives me the resolve to keep moving forward and do the things that provide me with the best possible outcome, despite the fear and uncertainty that might be present. We become more courageous by continuously doing even though the challenges are sometimes severe.

When we focus on the primary reason for being courageous despite the predicament we find ourselves in, we may find that it may become less challenging to exercise our spiritual courageous muscles. It might be easier for a father to be courageous for his daughter than for himself, or for a husband to be courageous for his wife rather than himself. Since the essence of Christianity is Jesus having the courage to do for us and not Himself, having someone else as the priority for our courage to move forward in a predicament is Christlike.

When we are in a financial predicament with a mountain of bills demanding our attention, it will take tremendous courage to do what is right in supporting the work of God with our finances, when we are also desperately in need of money. As I have said earlier, most people are in financial debt that they are not in a position to satisfy in the near future; however, God still requires all of us to have the courage to do the right thing in supporting the work of God with our tithe and offering whenever we have a financial increase.

Moving from big predicaments to big possibilities can be a reality sooner than later when we seek to do things God's way. Sometimes it is not how fast we get to the finish line that is the most important thing, but that we get there. There are lessons we can learn in a predicament that may prove invaluable when we get to a place of possibilities. The lessons along the journey may be just as important. It is not usually easy to wait, especially when we are asked to wait when things around us seem to be getting worse and more challenging every day. To be asked to wait when the bills are piling up and an eviction notice is on our front door after our car has already been repossessed is challenging. To be asked to wait when our health is deteriorating and the doctor says she is not sure what else to do is heart-wrenching. To be asked to wait when death has stolen away a loved one who meant so much to our survival, our future and the well-being of so many others is difficult!

Predicaments present us with many questions, concerns and uncertainties that, if we are not careful, can lead to depression, delusion and death. God is with us in the midst of our predicaments! He is willing to take us from where we are to endless possibilities. You may be in an extremely dark place right now, but God is able to let the light shine bright again on you.

Takeaways from Chapter 1

The answer to the all-important question, *How do you avoid struggling financially regardless of the amount of money you have:*

- ☐ God is aware of your situation. His desire is not to see you suffer; He will intervene on your behalf.

- ☐ The principle of stewardship was God's first assignment for humanity to be engaged in the garden of Eden even before sin. After sin, the principle of stewardship is still the number one thing God desires for us to master.

- ☐ Faith in God in the midst of a predicament is not a plea of desperation because everything else has failed us. It is believing that God is sovereign, omnipotent, omniscient and omnipresent. It is believing in God as the supreme creator and owner of the world and everything in it (Psalms 24:1).

- ☐ Acknowledging one's predicament and reaching out for the help necessary to address the situation is the first thing that will move a person from predicament to a greater possibility.

- ☐ We must seek God before we are in a predicament. When we do, we should be mindful that God may not provide the outcome the same way for us as He did for someone else. God's ways of responding to us are higher than our ways of thinking.

- ☐ Prayer is one of the most important spiritual resources we have when in a predicament.

- ☐ Having faith in God means that we believe God is more powerful than any situation we find ourselves in.

- ☐ Courage causes us to attempt to do things we never thought we would be willing to do and confront things we never thought we would dare take on.

Think about this:

God sometimes allows us to go through a predicament to learn to depend on Him and not on the things He has given us.

CHAPTER 2

The Big Deal

Am I a Giver or a Trader?

We received our federal tax refund about a month after filing. I looked at the additional money in our checking account and said, "Thank you, Lord!" I am now looking forward to the New York State tax return, to get the money owed to my family by the government. I filed for the state return when I requested the federal return, so I was expecting to receive the state return in a week or two. Several weeks passed and I was still waiting. "What's taking the state so long?" I wondered. I decided to call the state for an explanation for the delay. I was not anticipating this, but yes, much to my dismay, I was being audited. "Again!" I said disappointedly. Having been here before, I wondered if we were being audited again for the same reason. Yes, you guessed it, our charitable contribution once again grabbed the attention of the state auditors. Our charitable giving was a large number based on our income. Even though we sent a copy of the receipt we received from our local church treasurer listing all the checks we wrote, the auditors wanted to see some of the actual canceled checks we wrote to our church. The auditor remarked that based on our income, she found it hard to believe we gave that much money to the church. She wanted to ensure our contribution was indeed given as a gift and not for goods or services we received. I assured her that we give to our church and do not trade with it for anything.

When it comes to money, most of the people I know are usually very interested in the subject only when it comes to how much they can receive. They usually want to know how they can get the most money with the least amount of effort. There are those who are still interested in the subject even if they have to put out a tremendous amount of effort, providing that the return on their investment of hard work will yield an abundance of wealth. "How can I get more money?" This is a question that has motivated and directed the efforts of many generations. We have seen people do some things and have done some things ourselves that we would otherwise not do but for the sake of getting money.

Once we have received money, we often only want to exchange it for goods and services. To give away money is not something that comes very naturally for many people. There is usually some form of expectation associated with the giving away of money. Some people may want recognition for the money they gave away. Others may desire some kind of fringe benefit such as a building or a scholarship named in their honor, or it may be to lower their state and federal tax obligations (tax write-off). The idea of giving without receiving any kind of social, material or physical benefits is rare in the society that we live in. We live in a world that tells us there should be some tangible or intangible benefits from giving. Otherwise, we are seen as foolish, brainwashed, naive or ignorant for giving without having realistic expectations in return.

This attitude and mindset of expectations when we give have affected our relationship with giving to God or for His cause. It also may be one of the primary reasons people do not give more of their resources, including time and money, to God. Many people are reluctant to give "their" time and money because they do not expect to receive anything in return. In the last sentence, I put the word "their" in quotation marks because as we have mentioned before and will dive even deeper into it later, everything belongs to God. Why is there such a tension when it comes to giving? Why does giving not seem to be as embraced as receiving? In order to give we must first receive. Which implies that we must be given to in order to receive. Giving must take place first for us to have to give. The tension associated with giving and receiving is because we have incorrectly used the word giving.

I have the awesome privilege of traveling around portions of the Northeastern territory of the United States (New York City, Hudson Valley, New York, Western New York, Connecticut, Massachusetts and Rhode Island) to preach and teach about the many principles of stewardship. Whenever I am going to do a seminar presentation on the dynamics of giving, I usually like to begin with the following question: "Why is it that if I give you $50 and you take it to your favorite store in the mall it seems so little to buy most of the things you desire, but it seems so big if you should take the same $50 with you to church to give as offering?" The answers I have received usually echoed the sentiments that when you give $50 to the store at the mall you are leaving with something tangible and when you give the money at church you are not leaving with anything tangible. While that answer is somewhat plausible and indicates givers as valuing material possessions more than the supposed spiritual blessings we receive from giving to church, the real answer is much more basic. When we exchange money for goods or services at a store in the mall we are engaged in trading. Trading is an exchange of money for goods and services. Therefore, the store owner has the right to establish what the terms of the trade will be for the goods and services that are offered. In our society today, the cost of goods and services continuously increases, hence taking $50 to conduct any trade agreement will be very limited.

Giving in church is different from trading at the mall. So let me clarify something very important at this point. There is a difference between the concepts of giving and trading. Giving is to share or release something to someone without expecting anything in return. At the same time, trading is the release or sharing of something with someone with the expectation of receiving something in return. Many people who claim to give to church or God may really be establishing a trade agreement with God and not giving as they thought they were really doing. While it is true that God blesses those who give to him by giving back to them, the giver's purpose for giving is not motivated by what God will give in return, but instead based on their appreciation and love for God. He desires to find more givers in our churches and not traders.

We are never in a position to truly trade with God, even if we wanted to. In order to establish a trade both parties need to have and own something to trade with. The reality is, we do not have or own anything. Everything we have been entrusted with is given to us by God to be good stewards of. Hence, God has no one equal to trade with. God is looking for people who are willing to give bountifully and freely from what He has given to them.

The Bible teaches that God is not just looking for givers, but givers who are generous and cheerful. In 2 Corinthians 9:6-8 (KJV):

> "But this I say, He which soweth sparingly shall reap also sparingly; and he which soweth bountifully shall reap also bountifully. Every man according as he purposed in his heart, so let him give; not grudgingly, or of necessity: for God loveth a cheerful giver. And God is able to make all grace abound toward you; that ye, always having all sufficiency in all things, may abound to every good work."

It is important to note that the underlying principle we must pay attention to for us to experience the promise in this passage is motive. Our motive for giving the things we do is oftentimes more important than the actual experience we have from giving the things we do.

Charles Spurgeon once told a story of a king, a farmer and a nobleman.

> "Once upon a time there was a king who ruled over everything in the land. One day there was a gardener who grew an enormous carrot. He took it to his king and said, 'My lord, this is the greatest carrot I've ever grown, or will ever grow; therefore, I want to present it to you as a token of my love and respect for you.' The king was touched and discerned the man's heart, so as he turned to go, the king said, 'Wait! You are clearly a good steward of the earth. I want to give you a plot of land freely as a gift, so you can garden it all.' The gardener was amazed and delighted and went home rejoicing. But there was a nobleman at the king's court who overheard all this, and he said, 'My! If that is what you get for a carrot, what if you gave the King something better?' The next day the nobleman came before the king, and he was leading a handsome black stallion. He

bowed low and said, 'My lord, I breed horses, and this is the greatest horse I've ever bred or ever will; therefore, I want to present it to you as a token of my love and respect for you.' But the king discerned his heart and said, 'Thank you,' and took the horse and dismissed him. The noble man was perplexed, so the king said, 'Let me explain. That gardener was giving me the carrot, but you were giving yourself the horse.'[4]

Genuine giving must not only be bountiful, but also should be purposeful. When we are giving to the cause of God (offering or special donations) it should not be an afterthought. We should be intentional in our planning and prepare prayerfully what we will give to God's cause. This means that before leaving home for church, I should have prepared what I planned to give at the worship services I will be attending on that occasion. Similarly, this also means that if I am giving online or via local mail, I should take the time to prayerfully consider and plan for the amount I will be giving.

Purposeful giving also includes the reason for which I am giving. I believe the reason we are giving to a cause is even more important than the amount we give. While we may not always have the amount we would like to give in support of a specific cause, our willingness to give whatever we can give because of our love for God and the blessings and benefits we believe the cause to which we are giving provides for others is of extreme importance. Our purpose for giving is to be a

---

4   https://matthewzcapps.com/2014/03/31/charles-spurgeons-the-carrot-and-the-horse/

blessing to others. When we have truly discovered our reason for giving, we would scarcely need someone to stand before us to motivate us to give. After we discover our purpose for giving, an intrinsic inspiration will well up inside us, motivating us to give.

Ultimately, God desires to help us become cheerful givers and not traders. Cheerful givers are people who find abundant joy in giving. The power of the Holy Spirit has transformed people who are cheerful givers. Giving is not a natural characteristic that is a part of our DNA. We are born with the propensity to be extremely selfish. For us to become cheerful givers we must experience a transformation of character. Simply, yet profoundly put, "we must be born again." Only by experiencing the new birth experience can we become cheerful givers. Without the born again, Holy Spirit controlled life, we cannot be the cheerful givers God desires us to be. While God has promised to bless cheerful givers, cheerful givers are not necessarily motivated by the promise of expected blessings, but by their love for God. They are truly givers and not traders.

I believe our churches have too many traders and too few givers. There are many blessings God has promised for generous givers that are still in the storerooms of heaven waiting to be poured out because there is an abundance of traders in our churches and too few givers. We also find that many church members mistakenly associate their returning of tithe to giving to God. The Bible teaches in Malachi 3:7-11 that the tithe belongs to God. Our sacred responsibility is to lovingly obey the commands of God and return what is rightfully His. When we return God's tithe, we demonstrate our loving obedience to God. We have not really given anything to God, we are simply returning to God what is His. Giving financially to God occurs after we have returned His tithe to Him. Let us also be mindful that "the earth is the Lord's and the fullness thereof, the world and they that dwell therein" (Psalms 24:1-2KJV).

God, who owns everything, is the giver of all good gifts. He gives to us because of His love for us. When we think of the many tremendous blessings we have received from God, we recognize our eternal indebtedness to Him. Our response to God should include our willingness to give Him everything we can because of our love for Him. God has given so much to us that we should consider it an honor to give anything to show our appreciation to God for all that He has done. We can never out give God.

Giving During Adversity

Giving from an abundance at any time is usually not such a difficult thing to do. While there might be some concern about how much we give from our abundance during a pandemic, many people can still give something without much fear and trepidation that they will be bankrupt in a few months. However, I would like to speak to the vast majority of people who do not consider their financial resources abundant before and during a pandemic. First, let me say that I believe there are many people who are blessed with an abundance of resources, but often do not consider themselves to have an abundance of financial resources when they compare what they have with others, or what they have and the lifestyle they lead. While attending seminary, I can remember one weekend we had a guest preacher speaking at one of the local campus churches. During lunch, he shared with us that on one occasion he traveled to an African country to do an evangelistic series of sermons and had an unusual experience. He reported that while walking around trying to get to know the country's people and culture a little better, he noticed a young man looking at him and following him everywhere he went. After trying to ignore that pair of eyes that seemed to be penetrating him all over the place, he decided to inquire for an explanation from his intense "admirer." So he said to the young man, "I noticed that you kept looking at me with an intense look on your face." The young man replied, to the pastor's astonishment, "Pastor, you are rich!" The pastor quickly said no and went on to explain that he was not rich. The young man explained that his reason for assuming the pastor was rich was based on the fact that the pastor was wearing a suit and a leather pair of shoes.

Sometimes we do not realize how financially blessed and privileged we are until someone who is less fortunate than we are points out just how wealthy we really are. We often compare ourselves with those who are blessed with an abundance of wealth that we do not have (increasingly so in the age of social media), and hence try to convince ourselves that we are not rich. We may not be able to give as much as others give; however, we still have responsibility to give according to how we have been blessed. As long as we continued receiving during the pandemic, we have had a responsibility to give! Whenever we refuse to give after we have received from God, we demonstrate an attitude of ingratitude. Despite the situation or circumstances that we may find ourselves in during a time of adversity, God expects us to consistently demonstrate our profound gratitude to Him by giving to others in need of support and help. We are to give to others especially during times of adversity, as God may be using us to be the answer to someone else's prayer. When we give during times of adversity, we are testifying that God still cares for His people during difficult times. We should always remember that when the question is asked, "Where was God during times of adversity?" The question is really directed toward us, we who are

God's representatives on earth. In other words, our prayers should include, "Use me, Lord, to be the gift that someone needs today and the answer to someone who is desperately praying for help." Charles R. Swindoll, in his book *Living Beyond The Daily Grind*, says:

> In these days of abundance and wealth, it is our tendency to become ungrateful and presumptuous. Affluence abounds in our American culture. Many a family has a driveway full of cars, a house full of gadgets, appliances, personal television sets and telephones, and a refrigerator full of food. Life isn't simply easy-going, it's downright luxurious! There is nothing wrong with having nice things...but there is everything wrong when nice things have us. Ingratitude and presumption can quickly rob our lives of generosity and humility.[5]

Giving should not only be done from a place of abundance. Abundance is a very relative term based on one's view of what it constitutes. If abundance for you means that which you have in excess after satisfying your basic needs and wants, then many people will never be in a position to give. If abundance means giving after you have satisfied all your major monthly bills, then many people will not be in a position to give any time soon. If abundance means giving based on a certain amount you have in savings, then giving will not be something you can be engaged in too often. Giving should

---

5   Charles R. Swindoll, Living Beyond the Daily Grind II (Carmel, New York: Guideposts, 1988), p. 276.

be done at all times based on the fact that we have already received. Even if it means that we will be sacrificially giving on some occasions for some cause, we should be in the habit of giving consistently. Giving should become second nature to the Christian believers if we truly believe that "it is more blessed to give than to receive" (Acts 20:35, KJV). Giving any amount consistently is more important than waiting for a time deemed abundance to make a one-time gift. We should not allow fear to cripple us from giving during times of adversity. We receive by faith during adversity, and we give by faith, believing that God will bless both the giver and the receiver.

Takeaways from Chapter 2

The answer to the all-important question *(How do you avoid struggling financially regardless of the amount of money you have?)*

- ☐ Become a Giver and not a Trader with God!

- ☐ God's desire is for us to be Givers, not Traders. Givers share what they have been given without expecting anything in return. Traders give with the expectation of receiving something in return.

- ☐ Our motives for giving are even more important than what we actually give. We should conscientiously plan what we will give, before doing so.

- ☐ Often our greatest challenge with money management is not about the amount we have, but rather how we manage what we have.

- ☐ As long as we have received, we are in a position to give at any time.

- ☐ Sometimes we do not realize how financially blessed and privileged we are until someone less fortunate than we are points out just how wealthy we really are.

- ☐ Our purpose for giving is to be a blessing to others. When we have truly discovered our reason for giving, we would scarcely need someone to stand before us to motivate us to give.

- ☐ God, who owns everything, is the giver of all good gifts. He gives to us because of His love for us.

Think about this:

Based on my attitude toward giving money to church or for religious/spiritual causes, am I trusting God with the money He has entrusted to me, or am I trusting the money He has given to me?

God can do anything He desires to do, including satisfying all of my financial needs.

CHAPTER 3

The Big Difference

Secret of a Successful Steward

I was sitting at the kitchen table one Saturday (Sabbath) morning about to have breakfast, when I noticed my wife was watching a video that seemed to grab her attention. As I settled down around my large bowl of oatmeal, she shared with me that there was a sermon she was listening to recently that she would like to continue listening to. She told me that the illustration the preacher used was fascinating and made his point with such clarity and power. As a preacher I am always interested in finding a good sermon illustration. The illustration was in the form of a video. The video began by showing smaller white dominoes falling progressively on larger white dominoes that would knock down the next domino until it eventually knocked down a very large domino. The point of the illustration was that a small habit that is practiced consistently will eventually become something big! I was captured by that illustration and was eager to hear the following sermon. The very first statement the preacher made arrested my attention immediately. He said, "Successful people are people who are willing to do things consistently, what other people are willing to do occasionally!" By the time he was finished explaining that idea for about five minutes, I was ready to hear everything else he had to say. His second point was, "Setting goals does not bring about results, regardless of how great and profound the goals may be, but rather having good systems in place that are utilized consistently will provide us with the desired results. We rise and fall to the level of the systems that we are utilizing."

As I reflected upon the profundity of the preacher's first two points in his sermon, I began thinking about the many webinars, seminars and other presentations that I have done and that I attended that emphasized strongly that the most successful thing people need to do in order to be successful is to set clear and attainable goals. I am convinced that the real issue in becoming successful is not relegated to the clarity and specificity of the goals I set, but in my willingness to consistently do what others do occasionally and having the appropriate systems in place to arrive at the desired goals. Similarly, I am convinced that when it comes to money, the real issue we are all faced with regardless of the amount of money we have is our willingness to do consistently what others are only willing to do occasionally.

Things that successful people do consistently:

- **Invest in Meaningful Relationships**

    One of the first things that often comes to mind when we first hear the word *invest* is money. For many of us our minds take us to our bank accounts, and we begin to think about how much, if any, money we have that we can invest. We begin asking ourselves questions like: How much money will we make on our initial investment? How long will it take for us to double our investment? How risky or safe is this investment going to be? While it is true that monetary investments are one of the important vehicles we travel in to become financially stable, there are some prerequisite investments that must take place in order for us to achieve our financial goals.

Before we examine some of these other investments that are of extreme importance to our overall success, we need to establish a working definition for the word investment that we are using as the basis for our discussion in this chapter. To invest is to allocate resources with the hope of receiving a greater return than what was originally given. All resources are invested for a given period of time. Even time as a resource is given to us for a certain duration. Time is one of the most important resources available to us that requires keen investment for us to accomplish our desired goals in life. Time is given to us from the moment we were conceived in our mothers' wombs. Time is a precious gift from God that we ought to demonstrate by the decisions we make daily that we are grateful for every moment we receive. I have often heard the phrase "time is money and money is time," implying that time is a measure of efficiency. The less time taken to complete a certain task well means the more productive a person is. Our stewardship of time strongly impacts our financial resources. What, when, where and how we manage our time will determine how financially successful we are. Successful people consistently invest in the time necessary to achieve their goals. This may mean spending several hours initiating contacts, doing follow-ups, doing the necessary research, trying different approaches, and the list goes on and on. Successful people are willing to invest the time necessary for as long as it takes to accomplish their goals.

In their book *First Things First*, Stephen R. Covey, A. Roger Merrill and Rebecca R. Merrill say: "We're constantly making choices about the way we spend our time, from the major seasons to the individual moments in our lives. We're also living with the consequences of those choices. And many of us don't like those consequences, especially when we feel there's a gap between how we're spending our time and what we feel is deeply important in our lives."[6] One of the great benefits of investment in time is that it often provides the basis for new and meaningful relationships for the future. Strong relationships take time to build. This is also true when building an intimate relationship with God; we build trust and commitment only after spending quality and quantity time with God. However, it is a good reminder at this point in our discussion, to underscore the essence of what it means to be a successful steward: to be in the right relationship with God! Every good steward knows it takes time to be in an intimate relationship with God, as with any successful or meaningful relationship that we have.

I believe one of the first assignments given to humanity by God, to be good stewards of all the resources in the garden of Eden, was an indication of how important stewardship of time is to God. As a matter of fact, at the second coming of Jesus, the distinction between the lost and the saved is really determined by the choices a person made consistently with how they managed the time they were given. Our priorities in life will determine how we invest or spend our time. Soloman, the wisest man who ever lived, in the Book of Ecclesiastes 3:1(KJV), says, "To everything there is a season, and a time to every purpose under the heaven." Charles Caldwell Ryrie,

---

6   Stephen R. Covey, A. Roger Merrill and Rebecca R. Merrill. First Things First (New York: NY, Simon and Schuster,1994), p. 17.

in commenting on this verse in the *Ryrie Study Bible*, says, "Solomon seems to be pondering the sovereign design of God and concludes that all the events in life are divinely appointed."[7] While everything is given by God, we must be alert to prioritize carefully in investing our time in the things that will not only provide for our temporal needs but our eternal needs as well. God gives us time to prepare ourselves and all those who come under our influence for eternity. While it is true that no one knows the exact Jesus' second coming, we are blessed with overwhelming evidence from Scripture, history, current events and forecasts of the future that Jesus' second coming to earth is very near. We are reminded in Scripture (Luke 19:13) that while we wait patiently for the second coming of Jesus, we should occupy or do those things that are meaningful to our existence until the time of Jesus' second coming. One of those meaningful things that we need to do with excellence is making good financial investments.

Financial investments are very important in addressing our social and spiritual needs. Again, we want to remind ourselves that when we speak on financial investments, we are speaking about allocating resources with the hope of receiving a greater return later than what was originally given. While saving periodically or systematically is a good practice that I would encourage everyone to be engaged in, interest-free savings are not real investments because there is no greater return than what was allocated originally. The Bible records in Matthew 25:14-30 a very intriguing parable by Jesus about financial investments. The parable teaches us three important

---

7   Charles Caldwell Ryrie, Th.D., Ph.D. Ryrie Study Bible: Expanded Edition (Chicago: Moody Press, 1994), p. 985.

truths about financial investments. The parable teaches us that *God is the owner, and we are the stewards of all the financial resources that we are encouraged to invest*. This means we are stewards of the money God gave us to invest. As such, much care should be taken in what, where, when, why and how we invest money that does not belong to us. When we invest money that belongs to God, it should be something that brings honor and glory to God. Investing in the work of God that seeks to proclaim the gospel of Jesus Christ should be the first thing we consider investing God's money into. Where we invest God's money also should be a place that seeks to promote the welfare of humanity. Places where the interests of our fellow human beings are treated with respect and dignity regardless of their ethnicity, gender, age, nationality or religious affiliations. The Bible teaches us in Luke 12:34 (KJV) that "where our treasure is, there will your heart be also." Where we invest our money indicates the place that brings us the most joy and satisfaction. We should always be mindful that hoarding the financial blessings that God has given to us for ourselves will result in us denying ourselves greater financial resources that God has available to be given to us. The question of "why" we should invest God's money is simply because that is what God expects of us. Investing the money given to us by God is for our benefits and the benefits of others. The question of how we should invest God's money is determined by the benefit we desire to receive and our view of God. If we desire to a great return on our investment, we will be willing to invest more. If we also view God as a loving and faithful father, we will take great care in investing His money wisely.

    The parable also teaches us that **God gives money to invest based on our abilities**. Most of us would like God to give us an abundance of money. We want God to "expand our financial borders" and "pour us down financial resources that we do not have enough room to receive." However, we would not give a seven-year-old with limited ability, experience and responsibility $1,000 to invest. We would be more inclined to give a 27-year-old the same $1,000 and expect that with life experience, ability and responsibility he or she would be able to make wiser financial investments. We may be similar in age and life experience but may not have the same financial ability to invest the same sum of money appropriately. God, who creates us, knows us intimately. He knows our abilities and decides how much he will give each of us to invest. Keeping in mind first that what we are investing does not belong to us, and trusting that God knows our abilities and will not put us in a position to fail, we should seek God's wisdom in investing what has been given to us, rather than complaining and comparing how much we have been given with others. Our skill level and maturity may differ, even at the same age. Again, while most of us may desire to have more money to invest from God, we need to ask ourselves the question: based on how I have invested the financial resources God has given to me, have I demonstrated based on my ability that I can manage and invest more money efficiently if given to me? Many people clamoring for more money from God have a long winding resume of woeful financial failures.

More time should be spent in reflecting on how we are managing what we have already been given, before we invest much time in acquiring more wealth. There is great danger in giving more financial resources to someone who cannot appropriately manage and invest those resources in meaningful ways. This danger includes using the financial resources given to enable behaviors that are detrimental to one's personal growth and development as well as the growth and development of others. While the intentions might be good and noble about what the financial investment is hoping to accomplish, someone not having the ability to discern flaws and/or weaknesses in someone who makes an impressive presentation that lacks substance and authenticity can easily fall prey to making poor investments just because they are not able to manage and invest the financial resources appropriately. This can be seen when money is inherited and the person inheriting it has no fundamental lesson on managing money.

Another very important lesson that this parable in Matthew 25:24-24 teaches is that ***our financial investment reflects our attitude toward God.*** *"But he that received one went and dogged in the earth, and hid his lord's money...Then he which had received the one talent came and said, Lord, I knew thee that thou art an hard man, reaping where thou hast not sown, and gathering where thou hast not strawed: and I was afraid, and went and hid thy talent in the earth: lo, there thou hast that is thine."* Did you notice that the servant who received one talent went and buried it, not because of the value or amount of money he received, but because of his attitude toward the master? The first reason he gave for doing so was because he saw the master "as a hard man." In other words, he is saying, I know that you are a harsh man. I know that you are very demanding. I know that you are a very difficult man to work with. It was not the amount of money he received that caused him to bury the master's money in the ground, but his opinion and attitude of the master. While he is entitled to his opinion, his action of burying the master's money was not his only option. The master pointed out to the servant that despite your opinion of me, "you could have at least put my money in the bank, so that I could have earned interest on it" (Matthew 25:27). We are also aware from the other two servants' attitudes toward the master in investing the talents they received, that they did not share the same view as the servant who received only one talent. This means that the real issue with the attitude of the servant who received one talent can be seen in the master's response to him. "You are lazy and good-for-nothing!" This sounds harsh, but something worth examining about our own postures.

Some of the questions this parable poses for us to examine are: What is our attitude toward God? Do we see God as harsh and difficult to work with? Our attitude toward God determines how we manage the resources He has given us. If we see God as harsh, demanding and difficult to work with, we may find ourselves doing like the servant who received one talent, "hiding it in the ground." Again, this is not based on the amount of talents a person received. If our attitude toward God is like that of the servant who received one talent, then if we received 2 or 5, or even 10 talents, it means that we will be digging large holes in the ground to bury them because of our attitude. The parable also reminds us that a reward will be given to us when the master returns to receive our stewardship of the resources He gave to us. Those whose attitude toward God motivates them to manage the resources entrusted to them in ways that yield more for the master will be given more by the master. Those who hid what the master gave them and do not have anything more to present to the master when he returns will lose what they were given.

The servant also gave us another reason for his warped attitude toward his master. He says, "I was afraid, and went and hid thy talent in the earth… (Matthew 25:25)." Fear is one of Satan's effective tools that he has been using to deceive humanity ever since he was cast out of heaven to the earth. There are many people who are guilty of fear for not doing what God has asked them to do. These fears range from the fear of failure to the fear of rejection, the fear of the unknown, the fear of change, the fear of death, and the list goes on and on. Fear has caused many people to miss out on great opportunities that could have transformed their lives forever.

Opportunities may include getting married and having a family or getting a new job in a new city across the country. Fear has caused many people to be enslaved to their past and others to their current circumstance. They are afraid to let go of the past despite how long it has been, and they refuse to try new adventures because they do not believe they can do more than they are currently doing. One of the main reasons we refuse to, or struggle to, keep God's commandment is fear. Bestselling author Harold S. Kushner, in his book *Conquering Fear – Living Boldly in an Uncertain World*, refers to fear as the "Eleventh Commandment: Don't Be Afraid."[8] Fear opposes faith and tells us that we cannot, even in the face of overwhelming evidence that we can. Fear paralyzes the Believer and causes gross inactivity.

Once again, we note that the servant's issue did not have anything to do with the amount of money he was entrusted with by his master, but his own personal flaws of character. Successful stewards overcome fear by studying and living by the word of God. In Psalm 27:1-3 (KJV), the Psalmist says, *"The Lord is my light and salvation; whom shall I fear? The Lord is the strength of my life; of whom shall I be afraid? When the wicked, even mine enemies and my foes, came upon me to eat up my flesh, they stumbled and fell. Thou a host should encamp against me, my heart shall not fear…"* The Psalmist is reminding us that to be a successful steward, we must overcome fear and invest the resources entrusted to us by the master. We overcome fear by developing unwavering faith in God. Please note that faith in God does not mean that we will always be protected from

---

8   Harold S. Kushner, Conquering Fear: Living Boldly in an Uncertain World (New York: Random House, Inc., 2009), p. 3.

dangers seen and unseen, but rather faith in God means that He will protect us in the midst of any kind of danger. It is my hope that as we seek to become good stewards of God's resources, we will conquer fear and invest the resources like the other two servants who received two and five talents, respectively, as told in the parable by Jesus. They were able to double their investments and pleased their master when he returned to them.

- **Invest in Meaningful Work Assignments**

When I think of work, several things come to mind. I think of performing a task with the promise of being compensated financially for the work done. At the time of the publishing of this book, I was working as the Planned Giving and Trust Services Director for the Northeastern Conference of Seventh-day Adventists. Prior to working in this capacity, I was privileged to work as the Stewardship Director for the same organization for five years, as well as one of the local pastors for over fifteen years, and as an internal auditor for two years. One of the greatest joys I experienced working as a pastor was engaging in the ritual of baptism. Baptismal services remind me of the true meaning associated with being called by God to be a pastor. It reminds me that the greatest blessing is to lead someone to accept Jesus as their Lord and Savior. Working as the Stewardship, Planned Giving, and Trust Services Director and as an internal auditor gave me the opportunity to encourage churches to practice good stewardship of all the things God has given to us. I found great meaning and value in doing these jobs, as I saw many lives being impacted positively. It is important for us to find value and meaning in our current work assignments that God has placed us or allowed us to be in. God expects us to use all the resources He has provided us with to do meaningful work.

In the parable of the talents, spoken of by Jesus in Matthew 25:14-30, all the servants were expected to use the resources given to them by their master to work. *"For the kingdom of heaven is as a man traveling into a far country, who called his own servants, and delivered them his goods..."* Notice with me that the master called his servants and gave each of them a different amount of money to work with. Servants are called to work. This is the very basic responsibility of a servant. A servant who refuses to work will be punished and/or eventually be sold for someone else that will perform the work that the master assigns to be done. Since a servant's obligation is to work for his or her master, it is imperative that servants work to the best of their abilities to remain in good standing with their masters. The word in the New Testament that is usually translated as "servant" actually means "slave." The connotation is that a person who was a slave was owned by a master. While there were different types of slaves during the New Testament era, household slaves, field slaves, and others called "stewards" because their responsibility was to manage the finances of their masters, all slaves had one thing in common, and that was some kind of work to perform.

Successful stewards understand that they are not their own. Throughout this book, you will hear this phrase repeated several times: God is the owner of all the stewards that He has entrusted resources. Successful stewards recognize that they have a responsibility to work with or manage the resources God has given to them in meaningful ways. All of us have been given resources like the servants in the parable based on our abilities. God expects those of us whom He has given many resources to: education, influence, money, time, special abilities and many other gifts, to do great work in using these resources to build up His kingdom. Our goal in using the resources God has given to us should be like that of the servants in the parable who received two and five talents, respectively. They doubled the resources they were given through meaningful work. This doubling of the resources suggests that they were conscientious workers who took pride in the work they did. God expects us not just to perform the work we have been assigned based on the resources we are given, but He expects us to perform our work at a high level of quality, dedication, and excellence.

Like most young and inexperienced pastors entering the pastoral ministry workforce, I was excited to begin working. After working as a co-evangelist for a six-week summer evangelism campaign series, I was assigned as the assistant pastor to a newly formed group of approximately 70 people to start a new church. These 70 people were not transplants from other churches who were re-baptized but 70 people who knew very little about the church that they were now members of. With a group of approximately seven experienced members from the mother church, we began working to teach the Bible, familiarizing the new members with church culture, protocol, and activities. I can remember teaching the tune of the songs to those assigned to sing hymns for our worship service and explaining to those assigned as deacons and deaconesses what their responsibilities were. While it was demanding work, it was rewarding and meaningful also. I witnessed the transformation and numerical growth of that small group of 70 to become 220 three years later. This result came about despite the limited resources that were available to the team assigned to work with me. While we had limited physical resources to work with, God blessed us abundantly with spiritual resources that we did not have the capacity to contain. God gave me the assignment to work with this new group of Believers, and it is still, to date, one of the most rewarding and meaningful work assignments I was privileged to perform.

- **Invest in a Meaningful Future**

Another lesson we learn from the parable Jesus told in Matthew 25:14-30 is the importance of investing in a meaningful future. In verse 19, the Bible says, "After a long time the Lord of those servants cometh, and reckoned with them." When the master returned, all three servants went to the master and told him what they had done with the money he had entrusted to their care. Notice that they were not surprised by the master's return. Their stewardship of the money they received implies that they were expecting the master to return someday. All three servants did not lose the money they were entrusted with because they knew that sometime in the future, the master would return, and they would need to give an account of their stewardship of the money. Their investments or actions indicated that they were concerned about what would happen in the future when the master returned. Two servants invested the money given to them and had a 100% increase in their investment. I can imagine that they were eagerly awaiting the master's return to present to him the results of their investments. One servant dug a hole in the earth and hid the resources given to him. This servant believed that giving back to the master what he received meant that his future with the master would be at least satisfying. It is clear from the master's response to the actions of his three servants that he expected and appreciated a return on his investment. He commended the two servants who had a 100% increase in their investments and invited them to be rulers in his kingdom. On the other hand, he condemned the unprofitable servant who buried his investment in the earth and banished him "into outer darkness: where there shall be weeping and gnashing of teeth."

What we do with the resources we are given by God will determine the future that we will experience. God will reward those who invest the resources given to them by giving them more resources and, more importantly, a secure future with Him. When Jesus returns to earth He will be coming back to recompense all of us for our stewardship of the resources He has given to us. While it is true that we all have been given money based on our capabilities, I believe that we all have been given other unique resources that can be used to build up the kingdom of God. Some of us are blessed with the talent of singing, teaching, baking, cooking, and the list goes on. I believe God expects us to use those talents and gifts to build up His kingdom. What we do with these resources will determine the future we are investing in. All of us need to do an inventory of the talents, gifts, and other resources God has given to us. Then we need to examine closely whether we are investing these resources into building up the kingdom of God or digging holes in the earth and hiding what God has given to us!

Takeaways from Chapter 3

The answer to the all-important question **(How do you avoid struggling financially regardless of the amount of money you have?)**

Become an Investor:
- ☐ **Invest in meaningful relationships.** Having an intimate relationship with God is the most important prerequisite to becoming a successful steward.

- ☐ **God is the real owner of all the financial resources we are entrusted with.** We are asked to be stewards of God's money. God entrusts us with His money.

- ☐ **Our financial investment is a reflection of our attitude toward God.** When we invest in the Kingdom of God, we are demonstrating our love and obedience to Him.

- ☐ **Invest in meaningful work assignments:** God has given us the gift and ability to work. We should work with the intention of bringing honor and glory to God at all times.

- ☐ **Invest in a meaningful future:** Our lives should be a demonstration of the future blessings we are anticipating. All the resources that we have received should be managed in a way that secures us a great future.

- ☐ **Fear** is one of Satan's effective tools that he has been using to deceive humanity ever since he was cast out of heaven to the earth.

- **Fear opposes faith** and tells us that we cannot, even in the face of overwhelming evidence, that we can. Fear paralyzes the Believer and causes gross inactivity.

- **Successful stewards** understand that they are not their own. God is the owner of the steward and all that He has blessed him/her with.

Think about this:

My success as a steward is not based on the resources I have, but rather on how I manage the resources entrusted unto me. You can be successful with little as well as with much.

Plan for the future,
but live in the present.

CHAPTER 4

The Big Discovery

Untapped Resources

I met Sharlene, a wife, and mother of three young adult children, about seven years ago. She is a certified teacher by profession and has been working in the education field for almost twenty years. She enjoys her job and is grateful for the compensation she receives from doing it. While not a professional chef, she is passionate and highly skilled at cooking and baking. What began as something that she enjoys doing has grown quickly into a catering business. Sharlene shared that she discovered she had tremendous talent in the kitchen during her teenage years. "I love cooking and hope to open a restaurant someday soon," she said to me confidently.

A teacher by profession, she is a talented chef who is able to provide herself and her family with a supplemental income that is sometimes equal to and more than she earned biweekly from her profession. If she did not tap into the special skills and ability that she was entrusted with by God, she would be significantly limiting her earning potential to what she earns from her profession. There are many people reading Sharlene's story who can identify with her. Professionals who are also talented in areas outside of their professions could be a great source of supplemental income. Still, there are others who have not yet discovered all the talents that God has given to them. It is my hope in this chapter that the reader may reflect and/or begin to explore the many varied skills, talents, and special abilities God has given to us. Sometimes we have so much on the inside of us that is ready to be tapped into. There are areas in our minds where we have buried some of the talents that God has given to us. Areas that need to be excavated to unlock the resources and talents that have been locked away too long. Our minds are sometimes like our homes. We have areas that we use frequently and other areas that we seldom use. We need to go digging for potential treasures in our minds.

Two of the most amazing places in our homes are our attics and garages. For many of us, the garage has been turned into our personal storage unit. This area of our homes is sometimes filled to capacity with many things that we do not remember that we even have. Our attics are oftentimes used as the dumping ground for stuff that we occasionally use, maybe during the special holidays each year. However, before too long, our attics and our garages are competing against each other for stuff that has not been used for the longest while. Since the stuff in our attics and garages is often forgotten about, we venture to acquire new stuff because we have convinced ourselves that we do not have the things we need.

The reality for many of us is that we already have so many resources at our disposal, not only in our garages and attics but also in our minds. Resources that we can use to provide ourselves with so much more wealth and opportunities that far exceed our current position. It is true that God has blessed all of us with talents or special gifts that we can use to be a blessing to ourselves and others. In order for us to maximize our abilities in using the talents that God has given to us, we must have a change in mindset from an employee to an employer. We must change our attitudes toward the special gifts that we have been given as only an asset to help someone else accomplish the full potential of their talent, and consider how we can own our gifts to establish and help ourselves accomplish our own success. In other words, we must explore how we can use our talents to create opportunities for ourselves to become employers and not just employees.

Some of us may be engaged in professional work that requires us to use the special talents that God has given to us. However, our profession does not always employ our talents and gifts. For example, an individual's profession may be a teacher, but her or his talent may be cooking and baking creative meals. C. Neil Strait, in his book *Stewardship Is More Than Time, Talent and Things,* says, *"Everyone has a gift or talent, just as everyone has 24 hours in a day. God gifted each person in order that everyone will fit somewhere into the mosaic of life. By using our gifts and talents, we are fulfilled, we feel needed, and, more importantly, we bring glory to our creator." The talents given to us by God are to be used in ways that bring glory and honor to His name. If they are not used accordingly, God will hold those individuals responsible for failure to tap into what they have been given.*

Therefore, there are three things we should be mindful of as we seek to explore how to utilize the untapped resources God has given to us.

- All resources are entrusted unto us by God to be used to honor Him.
- Resources are given not only to satisfy self but to be a blessing to others.
- Everyone will be held accountable for the resources received from God.

Our churches are filled with talented individuals. Individuals who, by utilizing their talents, could do so much more for themselves and the churches they attend. I did a survey of a church I pastored in New York City and discovered that from membership of almost 600 people, which included over 450 professionals, less than one percent of the members were self-employed or engaged in any other income stream outside of their full-time employment.

God has given us talents, and He is willing to teach us how to be good stewards of them. For us to become good stewards of the talent(s) we have received, we must develop an intimate, trusting relationship with God. We must believe that God is omniscient and can be trusted. This intimate, trusting relationship will give us victory over fear and help us to clarify our priorities as we seek to maximize all of our God-given talents and potential.

As we set forth to reap the benefits from the talents we have been given, we need to be mindful that we are blessed with talents to be a source of blessings for others. Freely we have received from God; freely, we must give to others as well. This does not mean that we cannot benefit financially from the talents we have been given, it means that we can share the talents at times without receiving any kind of personal benefit other than the joy of sharing. We are reminded in Acts 20:35 that "...it is more blessed to give than to receive."

We have a sacred responsibility to be good managers of the talents we have been given by God. So sacred that we will be held accountable by God for the way in which we govern ourselves and the resources we are given. We are reminded in the parable Jesus shares in Matthew 25 that God holds us accountable for the things He has given us. The parable reminds us that God is the owner of everything and that we are only stewards of the things He entrusted to us.

It is also the sole prerogative of God to determine what and how many talents we receive. This further implies that each person is responsible for the talents they have received. We please God when we demonstrate good stewardship of that which He has given unto us. Conversely, God is displeased with us when we fail to be the good stewards that He has called us to be.

While I do not believe that all of us are called to be business owners, I believe more of us need to have a change in mindset when it comes to managing the talents and resources that God has given to us. We may not be called to be business owners, but the main resource of the business being operated by someone else could come from the talents I provide. For example, if the resource that I provide is singing talent, I may not have the resources to establish a music studio or the money needed to promote my singing. However, I can partner with someone who has the resources that I need to utilize my talent for singing. Sometimes we could get a lot more done if we are diligent in seeking other people who can partner with us to establish ministry and business opportunities.

When we seek to utilize the talents that God has given to us, we may develop long-lasting, well-established ministries and businesses. One of the lessons we learn from the parable of the talents found in Matthew 25:14-30 is that God gives everyone talents according to our ability. This means that we have the capacity and the ability to manage the talents we are given to be a blessing to ourselves and others. The reality of this astounding truth brings to light the wealth of resources a church with a membership of two hundred members may possess.

As we begin to tap into the vast resources that occupy our pews each week, we will realize that God's church has no lack. The sentiments of the 23rd Psalm would be the tangible evidence and reality of our experience: "The Lord is my shepherd, I shall not want." God has truly given us all that we need. We need to spend more time asking God to help us develop the natural and cultivated abilities He has given to us. This does not mean that every skill and ability we have must be turned into a business or a ministry, but that we have enough available to us to take care of our basic needs and use them to glorify God. Whatever ministry or business God has called us to should be our first priority. We should be careful as we attempt to utilize the many skills and abilities we are given that we do not allow our primary calling to suffer as a result.

One question that is asked most often when I discuss the subject of talents and gifts in seminars and webinars is, "How do you know what your special gift or talent is?" This is an important question and one that we need to be clear about. Because someone likes or enjoys doing a particular activity, that does not mean they have discovered their special talent or gift. Here are some ways that I believe will help you in discovering what your spiritual and social gifts might be:

- **Take a spiritual and secular life assessment test**

    There are several tests available to take that may help you discover your spiritual and secular talents. The Myers-Briggs Type indicator is referenced by many as an excellent assessment test. These tests will identify recurring patterns of strengths and weaknesses. I took a spiritual assessment test once and found the general assessment at the end of the test to be quite accurate as I reflected on the things I knew about myself. If you are interested in doing a similar test, please contact Myers-Briggs at sales@assessments24x7.com.

- **Identify the things you are very good at doing**

    There are some things that you are very good at. Yes, all of us find it really easy to do some things very well that others struggle to do and may take twice as long as it takes us to do them. Do not take the things that you do well for granted. Take note of them and explore them carefully to see if they are more than just hobbies or spare time activities.

- **Reflect on the view others have of you**

    Listen to the positive and negative comments from those who know you very well. People who know us well may see things about us that we do not see in ourselves. There are some things that we are more skilled at than the average person, but we either do not recognize it, or we might minimize it. Ask the people who know you very well to give you their most honest opinion of you. Pay close attention to the things they often thank you for doing so well that you did not exert a whole lot of energy and effort to do.

- **Examine the areas of interest that you have**

    Look closely at the things you have an interest in. The books, songs, food, conversations, and places that you enjoy the most. Your genuine interest in some things may be a window into who you are and what you are good at. Look at the amount of time you invest in the things and places that you didn't even realize you spent so much time in.

I have a friend who is a gifted accountant who has been working in the field for over 20 years. She is so successful at her job that despite the downsizing and relocation of her job because of the pandemic, she was retained by the company she works for. In addition to her job, she began to explore other opportunities that she could use to obtain additional income. She wanted to do something that she enjoyed doing and had the talent to do well. Being married with three children, she began to explore all of her talents to develop a business she would dedicate the income from to her children's education.

As she thought back to her earlier days, she remembered that she was skilled in craft making and decided to explore making wreaths for doors. She made two wreaths, placed them on her front door, and posted pictures of her work on social media. She began receiving compliments and requests from friends to make some for them as well. The orders have been coming in faster than she expected, and she is forming her business as a registered Limited Liability Company (LLC).

She continues to work as a certified public accountant but enjoys using her talent to make beautiful wreaths in the evenings and on weekends. Her children's future of receiving a good education got brighter because she decided to invest some money, time, and energy into a special talent that God entrusted to her. God gives us all that we need. We need to use all that we have been given to God's name, honor, and glory. The results will be amazing!

Takeaways from Chapter 4

The answer to the all-important question **(How do you avoid struggling financially regardless of the amount of money you have?)**

Tap into the resources you have been uniquely blessed by God with. Use them to your advantage.

- ☐ God has provided everyone with a talent that can be used in a ministry and/or a business.
- ☐ Everyone has the capacity and the ability to use the talents given.
- ☐ Our churches would have no lack if more of the members tapped into the resources/talents they have been entrusted with by God.
- ☐ God gives us all that we need. We need to use all that we have been given to God's name, honor, and glory. The results will be amazing!
- ☐ Whatever ministry or business God has called us to should be our first priority. We should be careful as we attempt to utilize the many skills and abilities we are given that we do not allow our primary calling to suffer as a result.
- ☐ When we seek to utilize the talents God has given to us, we may develop long-lasting, well-established ministries and businesses.

- ☐ As we set forth to reap the benefits from the talents we have been given, we need to be mindful that we are blessed with talents to be a source of blessings for others.

- ☐ Everyone will be held accountable for the resources received from God.

Think about this:

Is there a "gold mine" or two within me that I have not scratched the surface of my mind to explore and excavate to enjoy the tremendous blessings that I am carrying around with me every day?

CHAPTER 5

The Big Breakthrough

Stop Struggling...Enjoy Living

I grew up in a Christian home, went to a Christian school at every level of education, and have many Christian friends. I have always gotten the strong impression from very early in life that financial struggles are synonymous with being a sincere Christian. The message conveyed to me implicitly and directly throughout my childhood through adulthood is that financial struggles help us to trust in God more than we would if we did not have the struggle. I agree with the premise that having a financial lack and knowing who to go to so that it can be addressed could create a relationship of dependence. This is the likelihood because, as human beings, we tend to go back to the places, things, and people that we can trust to relieve us of our wants, needs, and desires. However, that relationship of financial dependency does not mean that I have faith in God; it means I know who to go to when I need money. Faith in God is more than God giving me the money I need. Faith in God means that I trust God to take care of me, even when I do not get the money I want.

Being financially poor or struggling is not synonymous with being spiritual or godly. I believe that there are many people who are struggling financially and are not in an intimate relationship with God. I also believe there are many who are doing well financially and seemingly have a deep-rooted faith in God. I have heard people who believe that being poor is synonymous with receiving a curse from God, saying they are not willing to explore a relationship with God until they feel that the curse has been lifted. I believe that God's desire is for "everyone to prosper financially and otherwise and be in good health, even as our souls prosper" (3 John 1:2). I also believe that when the Bible speaks of us "...having life, and having it more abundantly" (John 10:10), that abundant life includes a life of financial security. In addition, all of the financial blessings promised in the Bible strongly suggest that God's intention is for us to enjoy a financially secure life while we wait on the second coming of Jesus. God does not find any joy in our struggles; His desire is for us to enjoy the gift of life He has given us to the fullest. This is the message that I have been privileged to share in the Northeast corridor of the United States over the past five years.

One of the benefits of traveling around the five states that comprise the Northeastern conference territory is meeting many people from various countries, cultures, and ethnicities. I met Janet, a single mother of five children, ages ranging from 9 to 26 years old, one Saturday afternoon after a stewardship presentation at her local church in Connecticut. She was once gainfully employed and took good care of herself and her children. Shortly after accepting Jesus Christ as Lord and Savior of her life, things began falling apart. Her estranged husband, who used to offer minimal support to the children, could no longer be found. She thought she could handle things effectively until she got the pink slip on her desk informing her that her services were no longer needed at the job she had been working for the last thirteen years. Soon the bills began piling up and her landlord decided that he heard enough promises and excuses; it was time for her to vacate the property she had called home for the last nine years. Her struggles were real! "Why is God allowing me to go through so much, so shortly after I gave my life to Him?" she often wondered.

With a few exceptions and changes to some of the details, unfortunately, Janet's story of severe struggle is a very familiar story for many Christians. Christianity has become synonymous with struggling. We have embraced struggling as such an integral part of Christianity that we have reinterpreted much of scripture so that it endorses our theology on struggling. Bible texts such as "Yea, and all that will live godly in Christ Jesus shall suffer persecution" (2 Timothy 3:12). Another well-misused text is Matthew 8:20, which says, "And Jesus saith unto him, 'The foxes have holes, and the birds of the air have nests; but the Son of man hath not where to lay his head.'" While, at a glance, these texts seem to be embracing hardship and struggling as a part of the experience of the Christian life, struggling is not the sum total of the Christian experience. The sum total of the Christian experience is abundance, peace, and joy. Abundant life is Jesus' promise to those who accept Him as Lord and Savior of their lives.

I have discovered from traveling around the Northeastern territory of the United States that most of the people I encounter reported that they are having severe struggles with their finances. The report is usually presented in one of two ways:

(1) I don't have enough money to satisfy my needs.
(2) I have to work two and three jobs just to make ends meet.

Money just never seems to be enough, and as a result many people are struggling. Struggling to pay their bills of necessities, struggling to stay afloat, struggling to survive another month. If they don't have enough money to pay for the necessities, then giving money to the church and other charitable donations is unlikely.

- **Living Within Our Means**

    I agree that all of us could find a good use for some more money. We have a long laundry list of important things we could use some more money to address. So are most people really struggling because they don't have enough? Or are most people struggling because they have chosen to live outside of their means? I want to strongly suggest that most people are struggling because of the choices they have made. Choices that clearly indicate they are not living within their means. When I speak of "living within their means," I am referring to those people who make financial decisions that they do not have the finances to cover. These are people who make less than $1,000 per week and live like they are making $5,000 or more on a weekly basis. Their rent or mortgage is $2,500 to $3,000 per month, their car note is $500, and utilities (light, gas, water, telephone, and internet) average $600-$700 monthly. When you factor in the cost of food, clothing, transportation, and tuition, to list some more important things to most people, most people making $1,000 or less per week will struggle financially. Is this struggle really because they are not living within their means or a lack of faith?

- **Faith or Presumption**

    Christians are called to live by faith. However, there must be a basis for our faith. We believe God to come through for us because what we ask for will provide evidence of the sovereignty and omnipotence of God and not just me getting what I want, when, and how I want it. There must be a reason for faith. The pertinent question I need to answer is, "Am I trusting God to bless me with what I am asking for so that I can accomplish God's purpose for blessing me with what I have asked for?" There must be a desire to be blessed by God to satisfy a legitimate need that will bring honor and glory to God's name. What we ask for in faith should not only satisfy our desires for our selfish motives but also speak clearly of the power and goodness of God. God's desire is to provide for our needs and not to enable us to be reckless and presumptuous. Many people struggle financially because of presumption, recklessness, and lack of financial education regarding money management. They make poor decisions under the disguise of faith and are reckless in providing a stable environment for themselves and their families. They choose not to plan wisely based on the income they are receiving.

Budgeting

One of the principles of good money management is budgeting. What is budgeting? Budgeting is a determination made about how a person will use the money that they have received. This can be done formally by making a list of all expenses for a given period of time and allocating a sum of money toward each item. Many financial advisors will also recommend that savings also be included and treated like a regular bill to be paid periodically. Budgets should be realistic based on current and potential income. Whether the list is formally written out or mentally agreed on, failure to make a realistic budget can result in gross mismanagement of the resources we have.

Budgeting requires prioritization and planning. Prioritization determines what's most important, important, less important, and unimportant. One should be careful not to allow anyone else's list of priorities to influence their own. While all Christians should make God their first priority in their finances, the amount given above the required 10% tithe is a reflection of the love, value, and importance that God has to that individual. After budgeting what you have decided to return and give for the cause of God, the priorities of family and self-care, housing, entertainment, and all others are determined based on what each individual decides.

- **Investments**

    One of the things we need to be most mindful of when it comes to deciding on new financial investments is to examine closely the importance of the current ones we make almost daily before making new ones. What we spend most of our money on reveals where we are making the greatest financial investments. Whether that thing that consumes most of our money is a mortgage, rent, or car note, all our other investments will be based on protecting or providing for these primary investments. While some may argue that these everyday living expenditures are just that and not major investments I believe that these "small" investments will determine what the larger ones will be. Most people have a predetermined standard of living that they would like to experience and would be willing to make certain investments that will facilitate their desire. Hence, pay close attention to the seemingly "small" investments, because they will influence the larger ones.

Making investments in financial products should be done under the supervision of a knowledgeable investor of the item(s) we are interested in investing in. Thorough research should always be done before serious consideration is given to any investments. This research includes not only depending on the knowledge and recommendations of experts but personal research from friends and colleagues who have made similar investments in the past. While it is usually true that "the higher the risks when investing means, the higher the results," much caution should be taken, especially when the basic everyday investments that a person makes for daily survival are at serious risk if the high-risk investments fail. Small secure investments have the same potential to make large sums of money as high-risk, high-results investments. The main difference in accomplishing the same result is time. If you are able to wait for longer periods of time to get the desired result of a high-risk investment, then my recommendation is to choose the lower-risk investments and wait.

Savings

I was doing a presentation at a church one Saturday afternoon on personal financial management, and the audience was in support of everything I was sharing until I mentioned the need for everyone to save regardless of their income. A nicely dressed lady in the front of the sanctuary, wearing a big hat, raised her hand, and before I could acknowledge her, she said, "Pastor, only people with lots of money can save in these hard times." As soon as she was finished speaking, a man in the back of the sanctuary stood up and said, "Pastor, most of the people in this church are not professionals, we are regular people working hourly paid kinds of jobs." When he sat down, I asked him if he was implying that as a result of their income, they were not able to save, and he said, "Most definitely not." Before I was able to go further in the discussion about the importance and need for saving by everyone regardless of income, several people chimed in, most echoing the sentiments that savings was not an option that they could seriously consider at this time. A few people who supported the idea that savings are an option for everyone regardless of income.

I strongly advocate savings regardless of income for everyone. There are three things that we should consider when we are planning to start savings. The first is saving is not determined necessarily by income, but by the choices we make with our income. This takes me back to the previous sections on living within our means and budgeting. The choices we make about how we want to live within our means, as well as being disciplined with the realistic budget we have made, will allow us the room to save.

The second thing we need to consider is a realistic amount that we would like to save weekly or monthly based on our income stream. Saving an amount that is manageable will provide us with resources that will be much appreciated at a given time. While saving a small amount each month may seem too insignificant to some, the discipline of savings is planning for the future certainties and uncertainties of life. I remember when I was saving to buy my first car (pre-owned). It was a 1983 Toyota Celica that cost $3,500. While the cost sounds relatively inexpensive, in 1991, when I was trying to purchase it, my biweekly paycheck was less than $300. Buying the car was not the only financial responsibility I had at the time; as a matter of fact, there were other things that were much higher on my list of priorities. However, being disciplined and determined to save to achieve my goal of obtaining the car meant that I had to deny myself certain things to obtain my goal. After several months I was able to purchase my first car by putting aside a small amount each month. The amount did not feel like a huge amount each pay period, but over time, it accumulated to a point where I could afford the car.

Another important aspect of savings is consistency. I was able to buy my first car much sooner than many of my family and friends expected because I consistently saved over a period of several months. When we plan to start saving, it is very important that we also make a commitment to save consistently at all costs. There are many blessings that we deny ourselves because we are not willing to be consistent in doing the things that are required to achieve our desired results. Consistency in savings is as important as the decision to save.

Takeaways from Chapter 5

The answer to the all-important question *(How do you avoid struggling financially regardless of the amount of money you have?)*

- ☐ Live within your means, establish a realistic budget and save consistently.

- ☐ God desires that we enjoy life and not struggle through life.

- ☐ Poverty and struggle are not synonymous with trust in God and spirituality.

- ☐ Our choices impact the quality of life we live more than the amount of money we receive in income each month.

- ☐ Exercising discipline, commitment, and consistency is strongly recommended over engaging in one-time, high-risk investments.

- ☐ Budgets need to be realistic and adhered to.

- ☐ God provides enough for us to trust Him regardless of the situation we find ourselves in.

- ☐ The inability to save usually indicates that a person is not living within their means.

☐ Being financially poor or struggling is not synonymous with being spiritual or godly. Neither is being financially secure an indication of one's spiritual connection with God.

Think about this:

Do I establish and live within the parameters of a personal budget? If not, why not?

Being a good steward is not relegated
only to good times.
Good stewards remain good because
even though their situations may change,
their God will never change.

CHAPTER 6

The Big Reward

What Does Our Giving Say About Our Relationship with God?

S everal years ago, I borrowed a handsaw from my neighbor. I used the handsaw on and off for several weeks. When I saw my neighbor, I would often inform him that I appreciated him lending it to me and that I would be finished with it soon. After finishing with it, I forgot to return it to my neighbor as promised several months earlier. One day I remembered and decided to return it to him. I saw him doing work in his backyard and told him that I had something to give him. He curiously asked me what I would like to give him. I told him jokingly that it was a surprise and that it was something I should have given him a long time ago. I went inside my house, placed the handsaw in a paper bag and then gave it to him. When he opened the bag, and saw his own handsaw, he said he had forgotten that he had loaned it to me. I apologized for keeping it for such a long time. Even though I had it for several months and he had forgotten that he had loaned it to me, the handsaw still belonged to him. When I returned it to him, I was really returning something that rightfully belonged to him. To be more accurate, I handed or returned to my neighbor something that really belonged to him. I did not give him something that I owned; I was simply returning what belonged to him.

- **What Really Is Giving?**

A definition of giving that I like to use is: sharing something with someone whom I did not have any obligations to share with. It is, therefore, a choice that I make because of a reason other than an obligation. I really did not give my neighbor a handsaw simply because I had an obligation to return what was rightfully his to him. We sometimes say that we give many things to God, but really we are simply returning something that belongs to God. Tithing is one such thing that I would consider that we return and not give to God. So, what does it really mean to give to God, who owns everything? In order for us to give to God, we must have first received from God. When God asks us to return a tithe and give an offering, what does that really mean?

Giving is not based on a required amount but rather according to how the Lord has blessed us. There is a difference between returning God's tithe and giving a free-will offering. Returning God's tithe is a specific requirement with a specific amount (10% of all our increase) that God has given to us. Giving a free-will offering is the amount I choose to give to God in addition to His tithe that is based on my love for God. Therefore, the amount I choose to give can be greater or less than what I returned as tithe. If my love for God grows, it would be expected that my willingness to give more offerings will also grow.

It is easier to give from our abundance, but sacrificially giving is an expression of our faith in God.

"For it is more blessed to give than to receive" (Acts 20:35). In order for us to give, we must first receive. Giving is a testimony that God has given to me. When I give, I am testifying that God has blessed me to be a blessing.

God does not give to us for us to boast about how much He has given to us. He gives to us so that we can have more to give to others.

Most of us would agree with this statement when it comes to knowledge. You would agree with me that the knowledge, wisdom, or understanding we have been blessed with would be a tremendous blessing if we share it with others. I believe you would also agree with me that the more educated we become, the more we should share what we have learned with others. The concept of sharing and giving what has been shared and given to us seems to be a no-brainer until we begin to talk about money. The irony is that education, knowledge, wisdom, and understanding are all more valuable and far more important than money itself, yet most people, it seems, would be more inclined to share and to give more of everything else except money.

God has made some wonderful promises to us when we engage in the blessings of giving. Luke 6:38 says, "Give, and it shall be given unto you; good measure, pressed down, and shaken together, and running over, shall men give into your bosom. For with the same measure that ye mete withal, it shall be measured to you again."

The first thing we are told in this verse is that there is a direct correlation between receiving when we are engaged in giving. "Give and it shall be given unto you." We receive from God as we give on God's behalf. The text further implies that if we would like to receive more from God, we must give more on behalf of God. So since this is simple and true, what are some of the possible reasons why so many people are not giving more money in church?

The greatest deterrent that most people experience when it comes to giving is fear. The fear that we may give away too much and therefore not have enough to do the things we would like to do. The fear that if we give we are limiting our chances of accomplishing the things we would like to attain. Fear has had a crippling effect on many well-intentioned people throughout history. The Rich Young Ruler intended to follow Jesus, but because he feared giving up money he went away sorrowful (Luke 18:18-30). God has called us to a relationship of faith, but many of us have allowed fear to ruin our relationship with God.

The depth of our relationship with God is oftentimes revealed in our willingness or unwillingness to give. The amount of time we give in studying and sharing the gospel is a reflection of the value and importance of the gospel to us. The amount of money we freely give to the cause of God is a direct reflection of the value, importance and love that we have for the cause of God. Once again, let me stress the point: giving is based not on a required amount but on how the Lord has blessed us.

- **Giving What Matters Most**

The biggest challenge that I believe many people have when it comes to giving is not the amount to give but rather the heart they are giving from. Before you decide on how much money to give to the cause of God, ask yourself this all-important question: have I given God my heart totally? What matters most is that we give our hearts totally to God before we begin discussing how much money we are going to give to Him. I realize from my own experience with God that when I respond to God from a heart of sincere gratitude to Him, there are no limits that I would put on myself with how much I am willing to give to Him or what I am willing to do for Him. Giving from a heart that has already been given to God means that my motive for giving is based on love for God and not merely a religious obligation.

Giving should always be from a heart of love. We can give without loving God, but we cannot be in love with God and not give to God. If we find ourselves struggling to give to the cause of God, one of the first things we should evaluate is our love relationship with God from the heart. We should not assume that our relationship with God remains the same always. We may be deeply in love with God one day and not as in love with Him the next day. Our relationship with God requires daily investment. Without a daily investment in our relationship with God, where we are asking Him to help us to totally surrender our hearts to Him, we may notice that our attitude toward God will change negatively from one day to the next. In order for us to remain in an attitude of giving from a heart of love, we must consistently do all the things that will enhance our relationship with God. By doing the things such as praying, studying the Bible, and sharing God with others, we will experience the long-term heart transformation that we are hoping for permanently. The goal is for us to be permanent givers, not seasonal givers.

- **Seasonal Giving**

The Christmas season is commonly referred to as the time of giving. It is the time when gift-giving is at an all-time high. Most people during this time enjoy giving. Unfortunately, this season of giving happens only once per year during the last month of the year. That means we would have to wait for 12 months before many of us would be in the "giving mood" again. Since many of us like to receive gifts, that is too long for us to wait to be in the mood to give and receive gifts. Therefore, we need to discover ways for us to find joy in giving more often. Since we often give gifts as an expression of our love for each other, we do not want to send the wrong message to our loved ones that we only think of them once per year.

Giving, however, is not always an expression of love. Sometimes we give from a sense of obligation and not love. We sometimes give because we believe we are expected to by virtue of who we are as Christians. There are times when we give because we would like those around us to know that we give. We are more concerned that it is known that we gave than the blessings someone will experience from our giving. Our purpose for giving is not based on love for God or our fellow men but on the recognition that we get from giving.

The Bible gives us several examples of those who have not given, not because they loved giving, but because they wanted to be loved for their giving. Acts 5 records the story of Ananias and Sapphira, two people who did not give because they loved to give but because they wanted to be loved for their selfish giving. In Luke 18:18-30, we have the account of the Rich Young Ruler. In this case we find a young man who was not willing to give up too much to follow Jesus, because he loved money more than he loved Jesus. We find another example of selfishly motivated giving in the gospel of Mark 12:41-44. Jesus made the point to His Disciples that a poor widow gave more than the rich because they gave from their abundance, but she gave all that she had because of her love for God.

However, when we truly love God, giving is a natural part of our experience as Christians. Our desire to give is motivated by our love for God. This means that we willingly give to the cause of God all the resources He has entrusted unto us. If we are not in love with God, we will find it very challenging to give to the cause of God. Therefore, our primary purpose when it comes to giving is for us to give our hearts to God first so that we can experience giving from a heart of love for God.

The Bible gives several examples of those who gave because of their love for God. In Acts 2:40-46, we have the record of the generosity of the Early Christian Church. "All the Believers shared all that they had in common, they sold their possessions and goods and divided them amongst themselves, so that everyone's needs were met." Their love for God and each other inspired their giving.

The experience of Zacchaeus is another remarkable example of giving from a heart of gratitude and love. Before his encounter with Jesus, Zacchaeus was a thief who cared only about himself (Luke 19:1-7). After accepting Jesus as Lord of his life, Zacchaeus gave half of his possessions to the poor and four times more than what he stole from those whom he overcharged on their taxes (Luke 19:8-10).

As Christians, we are encouraged to carefully observe the laws of God. We are keen on sharing with others the dictates of the law and encourage strict adherence to the law as such. It is important that we encourage and inspire others to fall in love with and give their hearts to Jesus so that what is practiced and observed is a result of a love relationship with God and not merely the satisfying of moral obligations based on our denominational teachings and understanding. Let us do what God has asked us to do in loving obedience and give because of our love for God.

- **Giving More Than Money**

Each day, there are 24 hours, 1,440 minutes, or 86,400 seconds, and every one of them is a precious gift from God. Time is something we feel we never have enough of, yet we give it away so easily. Someone once said, "Time is free, but it's priceless. You can't own it but you can use it. You can't keep it but you can spend it. Once you've lost it, you can never get it back."

Time is one of the most important gifts that God has given to us. From the time we are born until we die, God expects us and those who have influence over us to honor Him with the time He has given to us. Therefore we must make conscientious and prudent choices that will reflect our appreciation to God for every moment of time He has entrusted to us. God also expects us to spend at least one-seventh (1/7th) of the time He has given to us with Him each week in intimate communion.

I once worked for an organization where the workload was hectic and demanding. There were deadlines to meet that threatened everyone's job if they were not met. Many of my coworkers would work late on Friday evenings and sometimes on Saturdays in an attempt to meet these deadlines. A friend of mine once said that he wished he could attend church with me on Sabbaths, but he just did not have the time to give up an entire day from work, or an opportunity to make some more money on Saturdays. After sharing with him how I was able to manage my time to get the work done without staying late on Friday evenings or working on Saturdays, he decided that he would manage his time better to achieve more in less time. After a few more time management conversations, he was able to get more done in less time during the week and visited the Seventh-day Adventist Church in his neighborhood. We honor God by taking the time to be in intimate communion with Him each week. If we refuse to or cannot spend time with God each week for 24 hours, then it is a clear indication that we need to manage our time better.

When it comes to being stewards of the time that God has given us, God expects us to spend quality and quantity time with Him, our families, and ourselves. This balance of time management is important for the growth and maturity we desire to achieve as Christians. Relationships take time to build. If we do not invest the time in the aforementioned relationships, God will hold us accountable. Time to worship and time to work and fellowship are all important in the stewardship of time. In everything we do, we utilize this principle of Time. It takes time to do everything: planning, organizing, and executing ideas. Despite our best efforts, many people often report that they just don't have enough time to do the things they would like to do. Since it seems like we never have enough time to do the many things we would like to do, managing our time wisely is extremely important.

In one of the publications of our "Good Stewards" newsletter that my office produces on a quarterly basis, I asked several of our pastors to respond to the questions below:

- When it comes to the issue of TIME, it seems like everyone is so busy that most of the things we are asked to do in church, people often say they would do it, but they just don't have the time. What do you think is causing such a challenge today for our members to be able to have the time to do more for the church?

- Most of our church services are not well attended. People again often refer to the challenges they have with time to attend these services. What do you believe should be the motivation for people to be willing to make or sacrifice the time for these services?

- Do you believe that the time we spend in our personal devotional time with God has an impact on the time we are willing to engage in spiritual services, including witnessing for Him? Please explain.

- When time equals money or something else that is important to us, we make sure we invest the time in order to get the desired results. Do you believe that because church attendance and church work are primarily voluntary activities, that's the reason many people are not willing to invest much time in church activities? Please explain.

- What do you believe you, as the pastor of the _____(name of church), can do more to inspire or motivate your members to be willing to manage our time better so that we can use our time better for God?

- How much time do you spend each week on church-related things versus family-related things? Are you satisfied with the time you are investing each week? Please explain.

- This church has some specific needs and challenges. What specifically do you believe we should invest most of our time in, to address those needs and challenges?

The responses I received strongly suggest that better time management is definitely needed by both pastors and parishioners. Spending more time with family and friends is one of the most desired goals of many clergy. In addition, spending time with God for personal growth and development is also one of the greatest needs.

- **Giving Back the "Goods"**

One of the amazing things I have discovered from traveling around to several churches is the wealth of talented individuals who attend our churches each week. I was always aware that our churches are saturated with professionals from varied disciplines, but I realized that our professions and our talents are not necessarily the same.

Our professions are the work that we are engaged in daily to earn an honest living, while our talents are those special abilities that we receive from God, which enable us to do a task or perform an activity exceptionally well. Therefore, an individual's profession may be a teacher, but their talent could be cooking. While all of our churches are filled with talented individuals, many of our churches are not utilizing the abundance of varied talents that sit on the pews each week.

Talent is one of the core principles of stewardship; however, it is one of the most underutilized principles in most of our churches. God expects us to utilize the talents He has given to us to glorify His name. Using our talents for God also creates an opportunity for us to be blessed as well. Our talents can be used to generate additional income, as well as a ministry that can address the needs of others.

I have asked all of our Stewardship leaders to create a registry of all the talents in their respective churches. After the registry is completed, each of our Directors is asked to share their registry with the other churches in that area. Each church is then asked to submit a copy of its registry to the Northeastern Conference Stewardship Department's office so that the entire constituent and areas can benefit from it.

I believe it's time we begin to fully utilize all of the talents that God has given to our churches. Our churches will be reservoirs of ministries, and our members will be able to be blessed individually from these additional business plans and ministries.

Giving for the Wrong Reasons

I grew up in church hearing the Elders who did the offertory during the Divine worship service emphasizing the importance of the church returning tithe and giving a liberal offering. Sometimes I would hear the Elders reminding the church that the tithe should be returned to God because it is holy. Other times I would hear that the tithe ought to be returned because it is a command from God. However, I remembered most for us to return the tithe to God, because if we did not, we would be cursed.

When it came time to encourage the church to give a generous offering, I would hear things like: We need money to pay for the utilities and to buy supplies for the church. We need money for building renovation projects around the church. I have been to camp meetings, conventions, and other large gatherings where the appeal for the offering was based on the overhead expenses incurred to have the function. While all of these uses of the offering are practical and necessary, should we be giving our offering because of the necessity that it will be addressing?

The reason I give an offering and what the offering is used for are not the same. In other words, my "why" (reason) and the "what" (action) are very different. II Corinthians 9:7 (KJV) says, "Every man according as he purposed in his heart, so let him give; not grudgingly, or of necessity: for God loveth a cheerful giver." This text reminds us that while we are encouraged to give, our giving should not be done grudgingly or out of necessity. Let us look at what giving "of necessity" looks like before we look at giving "grudgingly."

Necessity Giving

The aforementioned scripture says that we should not give based on necessity. In other words, our reason for giving should not be based on paying for the utilities at church, buying supplies, building renovation projects, or paying the musicians and the custodians. It should not be based on the amount needed to purchase the new church van, pay the Bible workers, pay the church administrative assistants, or purchase the books the Personal Ministry Department would like to give out to the community. As important, practical and necessary as these things are, the reason for giving a liberal offering should not be based upon the desire to satisfy these needs.

While it is important that all of the aforementioned necessities are addressed by the offering, the reason for giving the offering should be based on my gratitude and love for God because of who He is and what He has done, is doing, and will do for me. If giving an offering is based on gratitude and love for God, then I will always have a legitimate reason for giving. If giving is based on necessities, then I don't have to give because the necessities could be addressed by others whether or not I give.

Giving Grudgingly

We are also admonished not to give grudgingly. Grudgingly giving means to give reluctantly or unwillingly. It is to be forced to give or to give out of a sense of guilt. We are naturally selfish and, as a result, will find it challenging to give. Oftentimes we give grudgingly because when we look at our demanding financial obligations and our meager financial resources, we conclude that it is not possible for us to give anything.

We then respond to giving in fear and not in faith. We are fearful that God will not provide for our many unmet wants and needs. When we grudgingly give, we will not receive the blessings that God intended for us to receive. Grudgingly giving will be our natural response when it comes to giving if we are not convicted and converted by the Holy Ghost.

Seven Reasons We Ought to Give

Gratitude Giving:

Everything we have, we have been given. Life, wisdom, understanding, abilities, skills, education, money, family, friends, and the list goes on were given to us by God. Our ability to give therefore means that we should first be thankful for that which we have received and give to show just how appreciative and grateful we are for what we have been blessed with. If, as church members, we were challenged and encouraged to give based on how thankful we are, not just for the things God has given to us, but for God giving Jesus to us also, I believe we would be blessed with significantly more offering than we currently give on a weekly basis.

The Bible tells us in Exodus 36:1-6 that the people of Israel gave much more offerings than was needed to build the Sanctuary that God requested of them. I believe they gave much more than was needed because of their gratitude and appreciation to God for all that He had done for them. I believe they were particularly grateful for the 10th intervention that God used on their behalf to deliver them out of Egypt. The Bible says that Moses was commanded to tell the people to kill a lamb and put the blood on the lintels of their door post, and only those who were covered by the blood would be saved.

"The people gave much more than enough and had to be restrained from giving" because of their gratitude for the blood that was shed on their behalf.

Love Giving:

The Bible tells us in John 3:16 that God gave Jesus to humanity because of His love for us. Since God's motivation for giving Jesus was His love for us, we also should give our lives and all that God has entrusted unto us for the gospel's sake. We are commissioned to love one another and to treat each other with love (John 13:34). Our giving to each other and to the cause of God should be based on our love for others and our love for God. When giving is based on love, there is no numerical value that can be ascribed to what is given. Love-giving is priceless!

I have found in my love relationship with my wife and children that I am willing to give them more than I have. What I have is never enough for me to give to them. As much as I give to them, I wish I could always give them more. When we are truly in love with Jesus and the gospel of salvation, we will never be in a position where we believe we have given enough to the Lord. Our love for the Lord will always cause us to yearn to give more than we will ever have.

Grace Giving:

If all that we received was based on what we were entitled to receive, most of us would only have the basic necessities to live up to our teenage years. The reality for many of us is that 'basic necessities' is a very relative expression, and some of us would have very little to work with. Most of us have been blessed to have received far more than we deserve in life. The families we are a part of, the jobs we are blessed with, the houses we live in, and the cars we drive are only some of the many things that we can look at and declare that we truly have been given more than we deserve. God gives us unmerited gifts of blessings.

In response to the graciousness of God from whom we have received copious measures of blessings, we should also likewise give in the same manner. Grace giving is to give not what we think others deserve to get or based on what others are giving, but rather to give according to how we have been blessed. Grace giving is to give liberally without exactness or necessity.

Faith Giving:

Many people refuse to give when they have little or when they are not sure where the resource for the future will be coming from to satisfy the needs of tomorrow. Faith giving is giving based on what you believe about the Supplier and not based on the demands you have to meet. Many people miss out on receiving from God copious measures of blessings because they are fearful of the demands they have to meet, so they deny themselves the opportunity to give.

When we recognize that the Supplier of all that we need has endless resources, we will not fear the demands, but exercise faith in God, The Great Provider. Faith giving is not knowing what, when, where, or how God is going to provide for a need, but believing that God is still able despite our ignorance of how His sovereignty and power will be manifested before us.

Hope Giving:

To be confident that despite one's current situation, something favorable will be the result is to have hope. When the widow gave her last two coins for offering (Mark 12:41-44) despite the corruption of the church leadership of her days, she gave with the hope that despite how evil the Pharisees, scribes, and other leaders of the church may have been, her small gift would be able to make a big positive result.

It is important to note that God does not excuse the corrupt and unfaithful leadership of his church or any organization. However, our responsibility to give should not be based upon the leadership of the church or organization but based on our desire to see the work of God achieve the purpose for which God has ordained it to accomplish. Sometimes the journey to get to a desired destination will be difficult, but that does not mean that we should stop doing what we can do to ultimately see the desired result we are hoping for.

Joy Giving:

Whatever we do for the Lord, we should find joy in doing. To have a relationship with God means that we should be happy and experience joy. The prophet Nehemiah says, "The Joy of the Lord is my strength" (Nehemiah 8:10). In the Apostle Paul's letter to the Corinthians, he reminded the church that God does not want a reluctant and compulsive giver but rather a cheerful or joyous giver. God's desire is for us to experience joy in giving.

Giving should be an experience of gladness and delight. A time when we celebrate with rejoicing that God has been tremendously good to us. The joy that we experience in giving is from a deep internal place of contentment that is a result of knowing who God is. The joy that the Lord gives should be replicated by us in our giving of all that has been entrusted unto us.

Peace Giving:

John 14:27 says, "Peace I leave with you; my peace I give you. I do not give to you as the world gives. Do not let your hearts be troubled, and do not be afraid." We live in a world of turmoil and trouble. The coronavirus pandemic was just another reminder that there are some troubles that we will experience that are out of our control. Jesus is giving us peace despite the pandemic and all other troubles that we might be experiencing.

When we give financially to support the gospel, we are giving so that people can experience the peace of God in the midst of a world in trouble. Peace giving is done so that those who are experiencing health, financial, social, emotional, or any kind of trouble can experience the peace of Jesus.

Three types of Givers:
- Reluctant Givers

    These are people who hesitate and are unwilling to give freely and abundantly. The story of the Rich Young Ruler found in Luke 18:18-27 is an example of a reluctant giver. The Bible records that when Jesus told the man to "sell all his goods and give the money to the poor… the man went away very sorrowful." He wanted to give but was not willing to give too much because he loved his riches more than he loved the poor.

- Compulsive Givers

    These are givers who give because they are commanded or forced to give. This is against a person's natural wishes and abilities. The story of Ananias and his wife Sapphira found in Acts 5:11 is an example of compulsive giving. The couple decided to give because they wanted to be honored and praised like others who gave in abundance. Their giving was done to impress others and not because they genuinely cared for others.

This type of giving was against their conscious wishes and desires.

- Cheerful Givers

    These are givers who believe that they were given to give. They enjoy giving of themselves and the things they have been given. Giving makes them happy as they make others happy. These givers are people who give in abundance because they have a generous spirit and are often people who appreciate Jesus for giving so much to them, even His life. People who are cheerful givers are usually people who have a relationship with Jesus. The story of Zacchaeus found in Luke 19:1-10 is a good example of a cheerful giver. After meeting Jesus, Zacchaeus was willing to give up half of his goods to the poor and would restore unto any person that he may have cheated four times as much as he stole from them.

Takeaways from Chapter 6

The answer to the all-important question **(How do you avoid struggling financially regardless of the amount of money you have?)**

Give from a heart of love for God. Give because you love, and you will love to give.

- ☐ Give what matters most, your heart, before "your" money.

- ☐ You can give without loving, but you cannot love without giving.

- ☐ Give your talents to God and see how He will bless you for doing so.

- ☐ Do not give for the wrong reason. Make your giving count for something.

- ☐ Time is one of the most important gifts God has given to us. From the time we are born until the time we die, God expects us and those who have influence over us to honor Him with the time He has given to us.

- ☐ When we are truly in love with God, giving is a natural part of our experience as Christians. Our desire to give is motivated by our love for God. This means that we willingly give to the cause of God all the resources He has entrusted unto us.

☐ As Christians, we need to do all the things we do based on our gratitude and love for God. If church members were challenged and encouraged to give based on our love for God, our offerings would be significantly more than we currently give on a weekly basis.

Think about this:

How generous are you in giving from the resources God has entrusted to you?

God does not bless us just to make us happy; He blesses us to make us a blessing.

CHAPTER 7

The Big Problem

A Deafening Silence from Many Pulpits on True Biblical Financial Stewardship

P ulpits are usually places from where you hear a lot, regardless of the denomination. Preachers on any given Saturday or Sunday morning have a lot to say about everything. From current events to ancient history, from politics to prophecies and everything in between, beside, below, and above, you will hear echoing from pulpits. At the same time, it is true that some of our pulpiters like preaching about some subjects more than others; it is important that truth and nothing but the truth be preached from all pulpits at all times. This point about preaching truth is extremely important because what the preacher says has a tremendous influence on the listeners. Even though I strongly believe that everyone ought to study the word of God for themselves, the reality is that many listeners live only by what the preacher says from the pulpit. Hence, preachers have a responsibility to preach the unadulterated truth of the word of God at all times with clarity, power, and conviction.

When listening to preaching on the subject of God and money, I have heard sermons that seem to focus on reminding people of the financial obligations the church has that they need to support. While all churches will always have some financial obligations at least monthly to address, I do not believe that preaching on the subject of money simply to motivate giving to pay for the church utilities and mortgage is what God intended for us to be doing when we step into the pulpit. I have also heard sermons on the subject of money that focused on the preacher's needs. Several years ago, there was a televangelist who told his church and the world that if he did not get a certain amount of money by a certain date, he would die. While I am not here to debate whether or not that was a message he received from the Lord, again I do not believe that when God asks preachers to address the subject of money, His intention is for the preacher to make others feel guilty in supporting a ministry so that the preacher's personal needs can be met. Recently, I heard a sermon on the subject of money, where the emphasis was on the giver's relationship with God. The preacher told the audience that giving money should be based on one's loving obedience and love relationship with God.

Many of you reading this book might be able to identify hearing a sermon on money that reminds you of one or more of the aforementioned perspectives. I have spoken to many of my Seventh-day Adventist colleagues about preaching on the subject of God and money and discovered that many are uncomfortable, reluctant, or unsure about how to preach a Christ-centered sermon addressing the subject of money that affirms, encourages, inspires, and celebrates the goodness of God. Many of my colleagues from the United States and other parts of the world share that they stay away from the subject because they do not want to be negatively labeled as "money hungry." Others share that their congregation consists largely of low and no-income elderly people, so they do not want to be insensitive by harping on the subject of money for an entire sermon.

These and other reasons have resulted in a virtual silence on the subject of God and money from many Seventh-day Adventist pulpits. This has created a major problem for many churches that find themselves struggling to find money to fund ministries in meaningful and effective ways. This is an unfortunate reality that many churches are experiencing because Jesus, who references money and wealth more than any other subject in the New Testament, the preachers of the modern era are hesitant to address the subject. As we prepare sermons to share with our parishioners, it is important that we ask the Holy Spirit's power to lead and guide us into all truths about all subjects—including money.

"After spending much time preparing the sermon each week, sometimes I can't wait to get the microphone in my hand to share what the Lord has given to me." This was the sentiment shared by a preacher at a recent Public Evangelism and Leadership Conference (PELC) at Oakwood University. A lay member standing nearby overheard the pastor's comment and chimed into the conversation. "After going through a hectic week at work, I can't wait to hear a good sermon on Sabbath." It's an awesome convergence of the pulpit and the pew of great anticipation and expectation to hear what God has to say each week.

As preachers, we have the awesome task of preparing and preaching an original, Christ-centered sermon each week. This is not always an easy undertaking. Sometimes we pray and go to our Bibles, and all the pages seem blank. Other times we struggle with clearly hearing what God is saying to us through the identified passage from which the sermon comes. We want to preach a better sermon than the good one we preached last week. We want to preach a sermon that will elicit a rousing response from the congregation, but what shall we preach on Sabbath? While we sometimes struggle to determine what the sermon will eventually be about each week, it is often clear in our minds what the sermon will not be about.

The sermon will not be about a subject that we are uncomfortable with or something that requires deeper studying that we just don't have the time to put in. The sermon will not be about the prophecies of Daniel and Revelation because there is just too much symbolism, types, and anti-types to navigate. The sermon will not be about tithe and offering or money management because… well, nobody wants to hear a sermon on giving money to God and the church. People are already struggling to "make ends meet." What am I going to preach this week? Maybe I should preach about something that is currently in the news, something that is now trending. Even after praying, sometimes we are still not clear about what to preach.

In my preparation to preach, I am often impressed to preach on a subject that is not necessarily my favorite topic or something that I am very familiar with. Yet, it is in those moments of uncertainty and sometimes unfamiliarity that I experienced some of God's greatest revelations of His word poured into my heart. Those moments when I pray and ask God for divine direction, I am led to a very unfamiliar passage or to a subject that I do not think I would choose. While I believe that many preachers wrestle with the text they are led to preach, I believe there are many who avoid and even dismiss the conviction that they are led to preach on some subjects, such as money. Once I was told by a preacher that he knows that many of his parishioners are struggling financially, so he does not want to put any more pressure on them about tithe and offering.

Another preacher said to me that he knows his parishioners are beaten up so badly by the devil each week, so when they come to church on Sabbaths, they need an encouraging word from the Lord. It is becoming more and more apparent that many preachers do not believe that preaching on the subject of money can be encouraging or uplifting.

The Silence

I have mentioned a few times before about traveling around the Northeastern territory of the United States for several years preaching about the spiritual relationship of tithing and offering between God and His church. Everywhere I have been, the same question is being asked, "Pastor, why is it that we are not hearing any sermons on financial stewardship from our pastors?" At a recent seminar with several of our stewardship leaders from across four regions of our Conference, the leaders reported that they could not remember the last time they heard their current or former pastors preach a sermon on financial stewardship. There seems to be a deafening silence from many of our pulpits across the North American territory on financial stewardship. What is ironic with this apparent drought of sermons on financial stewardship is that all of our churches and the Church headquarters reported that among their greatest needs at this time is finances to undertake the many ministry ideas, building renovations, and acquisition projects. There is obviously a great need for a lot of money in our churches, but once again, because of a severe lack of preaching about money and the impact it has on our relationship with God, our churches are denied the blessings God has in store for them.

Maybe the great disconnect between preaching about financial stewardship and acknowledging our need for money in our churches is the fear of being branded as a "prosperity preacher." Over the past 20 years, the Christian community outside of the Seventh-day Adventist Church has been preaching a lot about financial prosperity. Maybe Seventh-day Adventist pastors do not want to be accused of preaching a gospel of obtaining financial gains because "it was our season of prosperity." Maybe it's the same reason many preachers don't like to preach about Christmas or Easter during those respective times of the year because we do not want to be associated with preachers who celebrate a particular date and time as holy during those seasons. Some preachers and church leaders who have sought to take advantage of the generosity of church members and supporters.

I have heard other preachers telling their church members and supporters that if they sowed a certain financial seed in their ministries, God would give them back three- and fourfold more money than they gave to the churches. These and other misleading claims have caused many preachers and church leaders to stay away from addressing the subject of money in their churches. I believe that those whom God has called to ministry should not use the ministries God has called us to for selfish gains. We have a divine responsibility to preach the truth concerning money as it relates to our relationship with Jesus.

Maybe another reason for the deafening silence on financial stewardship from our SDA pulpits is due to our understanding of what it really is. I have spoken to many of our SDA preachers here in the Northeast whose view of financial stewardship is limited to the returning of tithe and, to an even lesser degree, giving a freewill offering. This understanding, of course, suggests that God is only interested in the monies we give to the church. Since this is the common perspective, many church members view tithe and offering as an obligation to fulfill—"a bill to pay"—and not an act of worship or a demonstration of gratitude to God. Many people, therefore, focus on where the tithe goes and not the spiritual relationship between the giver of the tithe and God. The reason we return tithe and where it goes to should be of very little consequence in our decision to give tithe in the first place. The same can be said about our offering. There is also a misconception by many people that our offering should be equal to or less than the tithe we return. Since our offering is a demonstration of our love for God, there is no limit (minimum or maximum) on the amount to be given. Financial stewardship, rightly understood, is the good management of all of the monetary resources God has blessed us with. That means that God is interested in our tithe, offering, and money we use for our personal use. I am glad that God is concerned about my personal use of money as well. That tells me that God's interest in me is personal.

Still, I believe the main reason for the deafening silence on financial stewardship from many of our pulpits is largely because of the disconnect in many preachers' understanding between our relationship with Jesus and the giving of offering and tithe. I can remember hearing one of my homiletics professors telling my class over and over again that when we stand up to preach, regardless of the occasion, "all roads must lead to the Cross." As preachers, our goal in preaching is to point and connect people to Jesus. This can and must be done when preaching financial stewardship. The reason we give our tithe and offering should be in response to Jesus giving His life on the cross at Calvary.

Throughout the New Testament Scripture, Jesus spoke about our relationship with money and its impact on our relationship with God. One of the strongest connections that Jesus made to demonstrate the deep intimacy that exists between humanity and money is recorded in the gospel of Matthew:

> *"Lay not up for yourselves treasures upon earth, where moth and rust doth corrupt, and where thieves break*

> *through and steal: But lay up for yourselves treasures in heaven, where neither moth nor rust doth corrupt, and where thieves do not break through nor steal: For where your treasure is, there will your heart be also"* (Matthew 6:19-21, KJV).

These verses are profound and glaring indicators of the status of our relationship with God at any given point in our lives. How we manage the monies entrusted to us speaks to the role, value, and importance of God in our lives versus money. If money becomes the preeminent factor in our lives while we are still engaged in various religious and doctrinal beliefs, our destiny would have already been determined. To ignore the importance of preaching about tithe, offering, and sound fiscal responsibility is to ignore our true existence as human beings. We cannot live without having to make financial decisions that have profound impacts on our lives presently and in the future.

In giving counsel to his young protégé Timothy, the Apostle Paul reminds him of the importance of having a clear biblical understanding of what it means to be a good steward of money. In 1Timothy 6, Paul states emphatically that Timothy, in his new role as a preacher and church leader, needs to be extremely careful about those who have accepted the gospel of Jesus as a means of obtaining financial wealth. In the same chapter, he further said to Timothy that "the love of money is the root of all evil." Paul, like Jesus, understood the tremendous impact that money has on the Believer. Therefore, he could not omit the subject of money from the list of the most important things to share with his young colleague. Paul's intention was not only to point out the flawed approach that some Christians had to wealth and money but also to encourage Timothy to preach and teach the liberating truth concerning money.

I can still vividly remember, as a young boy attending church, that there were some well-intentioned local Elders of my church who thought that money should not even be discussed during Bible class and definitely should not be preached about from the pulpit. That negative stigma that was associated with money made it difficult for the church to embrace money publicly as a tremendous gift from God. While we were not taught back then about how to become a good steward of money, we were always encouraged to bring our tithe and offering to the Lord. We were not taught about how to manage the money given to us by God in order for us to rightfully and consistently return God's tithe. As for the 90% that we have remaining after we have set our tithes apart, no one ever mentioned how we could manage that portion of money so that we can take care of our personal needs while giving our most generous offering that is supposed to be a reflection of our love for God.

Today, we do not hear many sermons or Bible class discussions on the subject of money, yet most churches would agree that their ability to provide many ministries effectively is based on how much money they have in the church treasury. Could it be, that as pastors, preachers, and church leaders, we have denied our churches the much-needed financial resources that are available from the pews because we are not taking the time to address the subject of money more often from our pulpits? I remember hearing a story of a man who had a horrible dream. He said, "I dreamed that the Lord took my Sabbath offering and multiplied it by ten, and this became my weekly income. In no time, I lost my color TV, had to give up my new car, and couldn't make my house payment. After all, what can a fellow do on $10 a week?"⁹ Could it be that many of the people who attend our churches for worship each week give little or no money because they do not fully understand the relationship between giving their offerings and their relationship with Jesus? I believe it is time we break the deafening silence on money and allow our churches to receive the blessings that God has in store for cheerful givers.

Breaking the Silence

The deafening silence from our pulpits can be broken as we carefully explore the relationship between financial stewardship and its impact on our relationship with God. You would agree with me that anything that has a significant impact on our lives is worth discussing. Another way to look at it is anything that Jesus discussed consistently, we should preach about often. Jesus told more parables directly about finances as they relate to the kingdom of God than any other subject He spoke about in the Bible. A careful study of most of the forty-six parables of Jesus will reveal some aspects of finance. This suggests that as preachers of the gospel of Jesus, we must preach about the subject that Jesus preached about most often.

Here are some valuable lessons that Jesus taught while preaching to the Believers who followed Him each day:

1. Jesus taught that one of the most rightful uses of money is to support the ministries of the church (Matthew 23:23; Mark 12:41-44; Luke 8:1-3). In Jesus' day, it was Herod's temple that addressed the needs of the entire community of Believers, and in ours, it is the

---

9   https://ministry127.com/resources/illustration/a-bad-dream

local church and the community of Believers as well. As preachers, we need not be apologetic in preaching about the importance of people giving money to support the local ministries of the church. Most sincere Christians would agree that this is one of the most legitimate uses of money. It is also the divine responsibility of preachers to educate the parishioners about this most worthy privilege that they should be engaged in every time they gather together for worship at their churches or places of worship. I was taught from an early age, very long before I began earning an income, that I should always take an offering with me when I am going to a worship service at my local church. It is a part of my preparation that I still continue to practice when I am planning to attend a worship service. When we preach about financial support to local church ministries, we are helping our members to invest in themselves and the generations to come. We are also fostering a community of selfless Believers who will find joy in giving more of themselves, their time, and talents and all other resources.

2. Jesus taught us to use our financial possessions to meet essential family needs (Matthew 7:7-12; Mark 7:9-13; compare 1 Timothy 5:8 and 2 Thessalonians 3:7-10). After our responsibility and obligations to God, our next divine responsibility and obligations are to our families. The responsibility that we have been given to support the cause of God is as important as us giving and providing for our families' financial needs. When we address our families' financial needs, we are honoring God. Our love and responsibility for our families motivate us to ensure that their financial needs are satisfied. If we neglect this God-given responsibility, we

would be doing a great injustice to our families and find ourselves in a divine dilemma. Preachers need to remind parents and adults of this sacred responsibility that the Lord has bestowed upon them.

Money should be invested in our families that addresses at least the basic necessities of life: food, clothing, and shelter. After our financial obligations to God are satisfied, care should be taken to ensure that our families' financial needs are satisfied before anything else. Money should not only be spent on the basic necessities of the family but also on entertainment, vacations, and other areas of refreshments and relaxation for the family. When the subject of money management to meet our families' financial needs is preached from the pulpit, the morale and the commitment of the families that make up our churches will vastly be improved.

3. Jesus taught that we should use our financial resources to help the poor and needy through benevolence (Luke 10:29-37; 18:18-25). This is another important aspect of giving money that, as preachers, we need to preach about often from our pulpits. When preaching about giving for the poor and less fortunate it should be undergirded by love. We are encouraging people to give from a heart of love and because of their love for others. We need to emphasize that giving to the poor and less fortunate, is not limited to the treasury department of our church disbursing monies to people based on the directives from the church board. Giving should be encouraged to be done privately between church members as well. I would also like to emphasize here that giving should be strongly encouraged and not loans between members. Despite the enormity of the need, giving and not loaning should be encouraged. Loans that are not

repaid on time could result in severely damaging relationships between church members. Preaching about relationships between each other in our churches is something that we commonly do; however, we often address a large number of things that are destroying the relationship between church members, except the monetary transactions between members. More relationships are ruined in our churches because of unpaid loans. The intention was good when one church member was asked by another who was in need to loan him or her some money, but as the common saying goes, "The road to hell is full of good intentions." People are trying to help the poor and needy in our churches, and they need guidance from the pulpit so that good relationships are not destroyed. It is also very important that the poor and needy are also taught from the pulpit about the resources available to them to address their financial needs adequately. If the pulpit remains silent on the issue of addressing the financial needs of the poor and needy, we will do our churches a great disservice.

4. Jesus taught that we should practice conscientious financial management and exercise astute wisdom prior to making any purchase (Luke 14:28-30). We often emphasize that 10% of all the income we receive belongs to God as tithe and that we should consider giving another 5-10% as a freewill offering. Not much is said from the pulpit about how the remaining balance of our income should be managed. I would like to strongly suggest that much more needs to be preached from our pulpits about what is used for our domestic needs. Preachers need to remind their parishioners that they should seek divine wisdom in determining

what they spend money to purchase. Care should be taken when purchasing items for ourselves to avoid frivolous spending. It is also more important to purchase items of superior quality that may cost more initially than items of inferior quality that may cost less but also do not last as long as items of superior quality. If parishioners are not conscientious money managers and do not exercise shrewd wisdom when purchasing items for their personal usage, they will be adversely affected when they are reminded of their financial obligations to God. They will find themselves in the position of having the desire to do good but not having the financial resources to satisfy their hearts' desires.

5. Jesus taught, particularly through his frequent illustrations of stewards (Matthew 25:14-30; Luke 16:1-13) and farming (Matthew 13:8, 23; John 4:34-38), that it is appropriate, and even expected by the Lord, to invest our resources for long-term gain and/or financial security. It is important to note that the Bible encourages Believers to engage in long-term financial investments. The church (the body of Christ) is equipped with many financial experts that can provide the education needed to inform those who are interested in investment opportunities. As preachers, we need to encourage our parishioners from the pulpit to utilize all of the blessings we have at our disposal. I believe that God has provided His church with many financial experts. People whom God has called to be a special blessing in educating His people to make informed financial decisions that will help us with our financial future. Could it be that one of the reasons our churches struggle financially is because we have not done enough from our pulpits to encourage our members to utilize the

financial experts amongst us who can educate us about long-term investments? If people are taught how to make smart long-term investments, our parishioners and by extension the church will benefit.

Jesus also taught that we ought to pay our taxes (Matthew 17:24-27; 22:17-22). Caesar was the emperor of an oppressive regime, but Jesus' followers, then and now, were called to show deference to the ruling authorities in matters that do not violate our Christian calling to be his witnesses (compare Acts 4:18-19 and Romans 13:1-8). We have a divine responsibility to demonstrate to the society we live in that, as Christians, we will honor our local and federal governments by paying our tax obligations. As Christians, we must demonstrate to the world that we are honest people with great integrity. If we choose not to be obedient to our financial obligations to the local and federal governments, we discredit our witness as Christians to the world. As preachers, we need to encourage our parishioners to do what is right even if the government does not embrace all of our beliefs and values. We must make it clear from our pulpits that, as Christians, we are law-abiding citizens, especially when honoring the law does not lead to us compromising the laws of God.

The fact that Jesus, directly and indirectly, preached and taught extensively about financial stewardship from the temple, the synagogue, the mountainsides and everywhere else that He had an opportunity to do so means that we too, much more than any other subject in his three-and-a-half-year public ministry, should definitely go and do likewise. Jesus is our best and perfect example. We can confidently preach and teach the message of stewardship because it is the message of Jesus.

Takeaways from Chapter 7

The answer to the all-important question **(How do you avoid struggling financially regardless of the amount of money you have?)**

Preach and teach the message of stewardship with confidence from every pulpit. People need to hear and know that stewardship is the message of Jesus.

- ☐ The preacher who is reluctant to preach about the relationship between money and salvation needs to address his own relationship with God about money, to discover what is causing the reluctance.

- ☐ Jesus taught and made references to money more than he did about faith and prayer.

- ☐ There is obviously a great need for a lot of money in our churches, but because of a severe lack of preaching about money and the impact it has on our relationship with God, our churches are denied the blessings God has in store for them.

- ☐ Jesus taught that we should practice conscientious financial management and exercise astute wisdom before to making any purchase.

- ☐ People are trying to help the poor and needy in our churches, and they need guidance from the pulpit so that good relationships are not destroyed in the process of helping.

☐ After our financial obligations to God are satisfied, care should be taken to ensure that our families' financial needs are satisfied before anything else is addressed.

Think about this:

How comfortable are you preaching and teaching about financial stewardship? Is your comfort level impeding or inspiring you to preach on the subject of stewardship?

Preach and teach the message of stewardship with confidence from every pulpit.

CHAPTER 8

The Big Truth

Our Churches Need Our Offerings

Tim Challies, in his article "Seven Things Your Church Needs From You," says these things are:

- Being Humble
- Prioritizing Church
- Giving God a Day
- Living Like a Christian All Week
- Getting to Know People Not Like You
- Learning Generosity
- Being a Great Church Member

Challies argues that when a person gives these seven things priority, the Church will be a better and stronger entity to meet the needs of its community.[10] I believe that as Christians, we should endeavor to give all seven things to our local churches.

Please note that of the seven things listed by Challies, only the principle of generosity is listed as something to be learned. While it is true that there is an element of learning that is required for all, giving generously in church goes against our nature. We are selfish by nature and can only become cheerful, generous givers if we have been "born again"! The old selfish person that I was before giving my life to Christ must be put to death. The new person that I am in Christ will learn to be a generous giver.

What does our giving say about our relationship with God?

Giving is not based on a required amount but on how the Lord has blessed us. There is a difference between returning God's tithe and giving a free-will offering. Returning God's tithe is a specific requirement with a specific amount (10% of all our increase) that God has given to us. Giving a free-will offering is the amount I choose to give to God in addition to His tithe that is based on my love for God. Therefore, the amount I choose to give can be greater or less than what I returned as tithe. If my love for God grows, it would be expected that my willingness to give more offerings will also grow.

---

10 https://www.challies.com/christian-living/7-things-your-church-needs-from-you/

It is easier to give from our abundance, but sacrificially giving is an expression of our faith in God.

"For it is more blessed to give than to receive"(Acts 20:35). In order for us to give, we must first receive. Giving is a testimony that God has given to me. When I give, I am testifying that God has blessed me to be a blessing.

God does not give to us for us to boast about how much He has given to us. He gives to us so that we can have more to give to others.

Most of us would agree with this statement when it comes to knowledge. You would agree with me that the knowledge, wisdom, or understanding we have been blessed with would be of tremendous blessings if we share it with others. I believe you would also agree with me that the more educated we become, the more we should share what we have learned with others. The concept of sharing and giving what has been shared and given to us seems to be a no-brainer until we begin to talk about money. The irony is that education, knowledge, wisdom, and understanding are all more valuable and far more important than money itself, yet most people, it seems, would be more inclined to share and give more of everything else except money.

God has made some "super promises" to us when we engage in the blessings of giving. Luke 6:38 says, "Give, and it shall be given unto you; good measure, pressed down, and shaken together, and running over, shall men give into your bosom. For with the same measure that ye mete withal, it shall be measured to you again."

The first thing we are told in this verse is that there is a direct correlation between receiving when we are engaged in giving. "Give, and it shall be given unto you." We receive from God as we give on God's behalf. The text further implies that if we would like to receive more from God, we must give more on behalf of God. So since this is simple and true, what are some of the possible reasons why so many people are not giving more money in church?

The depth of our relationship with God is often revealed in our willingness or unwillingness to give. The amount of time we give to studying and sharing the gospel is a reflection of the value and importance of the gospel to us. The amount of money we freely give to the cause of God is a direct reflection of the value, importance, and love that we have for the cause of God. Once again, let me stress the point: giving is based not on a required amount but according to how the Lord has blessed us.

Why Is Offering So Important to God?

An offering is a testimony of the financial blessings that God has bestowed upon us. Allow me to once again repeat this salient truth: we cannot give what we do not have! In the New Testament Book of Acts 3, this truth about only being able to give from what we have received is vividly portrayed. Three disciples were on their way to the temple for an afternoon prayer service when they met a man lame from birth lying on a mat close to the temple gate. The story says that when the man saw the disciples about to enter the temple, he asked them for some money. The disciples told the man to look at them, which the man did with great anticipation to receive money from them. However, to his great disappointment, Peter, one of the disciples, told the man that they had no money to give him. The disciples were not able to give the man any amount of money because they just did not have any money. They might have desired to give the man some money because of the desperate need that he had. They might have wished they had walked with some money as an offering that afternoon, that they could have given the man some money.

Regardless of their desire to give this man some money, the reality was that they had no money. They just could not give the man any amount of money, because they did not have any money. What they had to give was something even more powerful, more satisfying, than money. What they gave the man was a testimony of something that they already had prior to meeting the man. They gave him the healing power of the Holy Spirit. They gave what they had, not what they wished they had. God only asked us to give what He has provided us with. The disciples did not give the man a Bible study about the Holy Spirit's power. They gave the man a full measure of the miraculous healing power of the Holy Spirit. Likewise, we need to give our most generous offering from that which we have received from the Lord so that the ministries for which we give our offering can be fully blessed. The amount we give from what we have received is a reflection of the gratitude we are giving to the one who gave us in the first place.

Demonstration of Our Love for God

Giving our offerings is an act of worship before God. This means that the offerings we bring before the Lord should be carefully thought of and prepared ahead of time before the offering plates/baskets are brought before us. We are not searching in our pocketbooks and wallets for spare change to give as offerings. This last-minute attempt would suggest that we are giving to God whatever we can find and not what we intentionally planned to give to His service. Giving last minute does not demonstrate a true act of worship if we had time to prepare prior to the worship service. In counseling the Corinthian church, the Apostle Paul, says in his second Epistle, chapter 9:6, *"Every man according as he purposed in his heart, so let him give, not grudgingly, or of necessity: for God loveth a cheerful giver."* We have discussed this verse in detail before, but I would like to focus again on the first clause in the verse. The text states that giving should be purposeful. It should be done with intentionality and reason.

Our offering really should also be a demonstration of our love for God. In the gospel of John 3:16, we are told that what motivated God to give us Jesus as our atoning sacrifice for sin was His love for humanity. John 3:16 says, "For God so loved the world that He gave His only begotten son…" God's motive for giving the greatest offering for our redemption from sin was His love for us. Our love for God is revealed in our giving of offerings. How much we give should be based on how much we have been given. This means that an offering given based on love does not have a prescribed specific amount. The amount is determined by the generosity of the giver's heart based on how much he or she received. Giving an offering is an individual love response to God for the gift of salvation He has provided in giving Jesus as a ransom for sin. There is absolutely no amount that we can ever give that could satisfy the debt that was paid for our salvation. We give from a heart of gratitude and appreciation, not with the intent to pay off a debt, but only to continuously say thank you, Jesus, for what you have done for us.

Removal of Selfishness from Our Hearts

At the core of the malady of sin is selfishness. Our desire as we grow more and more to reflect the image of God each day is to overcome selfishness. God has instituted the blessing of giving financial offerings as one of the means to help us to overcome the issue of selfishness. Selfishness is something that every person has to overcome in order to be saved. The good news is that God is not asking us to do the impossible all by ourselves. Whatever God asks us to do, He is always willing to do with us, in us, and for us! He asks us to give a generous offering only because He has given us a generous financial blessing. A generous offering is not the same for everyone. Generosity is not a specific amount but rather a significant amount based on what you have received. The more we give, the more selfless we become. The more selfless we are, the more we become like Jesus. We ought to thank God for the ministry of giving that will help us to be ready to enter the eternal kingdom God has prepared for the faithful.

Giving Open Doors and Windows of Spiritual and Financial Blessings

One of my favorite promises in the Bible is found in Malachi 3:8-12 (KJV), which says,

> *"Will a man rob God? Yet ye have robbed me. But ye say, wherein have we robbed thee? In tithes and offerings. Ye are cursed with a curse: for ye have robbed me, even this whole nation. Bring ye all tithes into the storehouse, that there may be meat in mine house, and prove me now herewith, saith the Lord of hosts, if I will not open the windows of heaven, and pour you out such a blessing, that there shall not be room enough to receive it. And I will rebuke the devourer for your sakes, and he shall not destroy the fruits of your ground; neither shall your vine cast her fruit before the time in the field, saith the Lord of hosts. And all nations shall call you blessed: for ye shall be a delightsome land, saith the Lord of hosts."*

I may have quoted this promise earlier in previous chapters and will probably quote it again later on. This is such a great promise of financial and spiritual blessings that sometimes I am at a loss for words to express my gratitude to God for these verses of scripture. When I think about this promise associated with giving our offering and tithe, I am amazed with excitement and gratitude. God is promising me financial blessings that I will not have enough capacity to receive. How many people reading this promise believe that this is true? Not just an acknowledgment of the promise but truly believing that because of their love, faithfulness, and generosity to the cause of God, they will be blessed so abundantly that it will be more than they can manage! In addition to the financial blessings promised, God also promises spiritual blessings. The blessing to rebuke Satan and give us overcoming power to be faithful and generous givers is second to none. One of the greatest blessings we could ever receive is the blessing of overcoming Satan. That means that we would be able to do the things we need to do and refrain from doing the things we ought not to do. The promise further states that God will protect and provide for us all the food and drink that we need. When we cheerfully give our offerings, God gives back to us far more than we could ever ask for or imagine. We have the keys to unlock heaven's storehouse and keep the windows and doors of heaven open and pour down on us copious measures of blessings, or we can choose to close the windows and doors of heaven and deny ourselves tremendous blessings.

Giving Allows God to Act on Our Behalf

Throughout the Bible, we find that God is most interested in engaging us in a covenant relationship with Him. God is not merely interested in making us promises but in establishing covenants with us. A promise would simply be God saying that he would do something on our behalf without the obligation of any actions taken on our part. On the other hand, a covenant is a mutual agreement that God establishes with us that He will act favorably on our behalf if we are willing to respond to Him in loving obedience. God's covenants with us, rightly understood, involve God doing through us what He requires from us as well as Him doing for us. This means that even the act of obedience that God requires of us is something that we are only able to do because of God's working in and through us.

When we give our offerings to God, we are allowing God to do for us that which He has covenanted to do on our behalf. He wants to bless us abundantly with financial blessings. People often try to shy away from saying that God will bless us financially when we honor the covenant He has established with us, or they will equate only financial blessings as the result of us honoring the covenant relationship with God. I do not believe that financial blessings are always the result of us honoring our relationship with God. However, I do believe that financial blessings are part of the overall package of blessings that God gives to those who are faithful in honoring their covenant with Him. Financial blessings do not mean that the Believer should always be on the lookout for money; the blessing may manifest itself in the many ways that God has spared us from significant financial obligations. Other times we realize the financial blessings as God continues to bless what we already have to do so much more than we thought we could do. Since God cannot contradict Himself, He is not able to act on our behalf in ways that could bring copious measures of blessings in our lives if we are not willing to do the things that He requires of us to do. We must be careful that we are not the ones denying ourselves the blessings that God has in store for us.

You Can Give Without Loving, But You Can't Love Without Giving!

The Christmas season is commonly referred to as the time of giving. It is the time when gift-giving is at an all-time high. Most people during this time enjoy giving. Unfortunately, this season of giving happens only once per year during the last month of the year. That means we would have to wait for 12 months before many of us would be in the "giving mood" again. Since we all like to receive gifts, that is too long for us to wait to be in the mood to give and receive gifts. Therefore, we need to discover ways for us to find joy in giving more often. Since we often give gifts as an expression of our love for each other, we do not want to send the wrong message to our loved ones that we only think of them once per year.

Giving, however, is not always an expression of love. Sometimes we give from a sense of obligation and not love. We sometimes give because we believe it is expected of us to give by virtue of who we are as Christians. There are times when we give because we would like those around us to know that we give. We are more concerned that it is known that we gave than the blessings someone will experience from our giving. Our purpose for giving is not based on love for God or our fellow men but on the recognition that we get from giving.

The Bible gives us several examples of those who gave money not because they loved giving but because they wanted to be loved for their giving. Acts 5 records the story of Ananias and Sapphira, two people who gave money not because they loved to give but because they wanted to be loved for their selfish giving. In Luke 18:18-30, we have the account of the Rich Young Ruler. In this case we find a young man who was not willing to give up too much to follow Jesus, because he loved money more than he loved Jesus. We find another example of selfishly motivated giving in the gospel of Mark 12:41-44. Jesus made the point to His disciples that a poor widow gave more than the rich because they gave from their abundance, but she gave all that she had because of her love for God.

However, when we are truly love God, giving is a natural part of our experience as Christians. Our desire to give is motivated by our love for God. This means that we willingly give to the cause of God all the resources He has entrusted unto us. If we are not in love with God, we will find it very challenging to give to the cause of God. Therefore, our primary purpose when it comes to giving is for us to give our hearts to God first so that we can experience giving from a heart of love for God.

The Bible gives several examples of those who gave because of their love for God. In Acts 2:40-46, we have the record of the generosity of the Early Christian Church. "All the Believers shared all that they had in common; they sold their possessions and goods and divided them amongst themselves so that everyone's needs were met." Their love for each other inspired their giving to each other.

The experience of Zacchaeus is also another remarkable example of giving from a heart of gratitude and love. Before his encounter with Jesus, Zacchaeus was a thief who cared only about himself (Luke 19:1-7). After accepting Jesus as Lord of his life, Zacchaeus gave half of his possessions to the poor and four times more than what he stole from those whom he overcharged on their taxes (Luke 19:8-10).

As Seventh-day Adventist Christians, we make careful observations of the laws of God. We are keen on sharing with others the dictates of the law and encourage strict adherence to the law as such. It is important that we encourage and inspire others to fall in love with and give their hearts to Jesus so that what is practiced and observed is a result of a love relationship with God and not merely the satisfying of moral obligations based on our denominational teachings and understanding. Let us do and give because of our love for God.

Giving Not Based on Leadership

We return tithe and give our offerings to God. Regardless of how we may feel about our local church leadership, we have a divine obligation to return our tithe and offering to the church. The church may have faults and weaknesses; however, this system of giving to God is divinely established. While we may have disagreements with church leaders, we have a spiritual obligation to honor God in our tithe and offering. We may not agree with our local politicians or the leadership of our country, but we have a responsibility to pay taxes.

In Luke's gospel (21:41-44), we find an interesting incident involving worshipers giving their offering as they enter the courtyard of the temple for worship. The church leaders had constructed 13 "trumpet-like boxes" in the courtyard for women, which worshipers were asked to put their offerings. Now let me pause here and digress for a minute. The offering was Holy unto the Lord, and the church leaders chose not to put the offering boxes in the inner court where the "holy" men sat. They placed them where the women were allowed to sit. They wanted to make sure they got the offering from everyone, regardless of the restriction they placed on some worshipers. The Bible says that while Jesus sat there, He observed the worshipers putting their offerings in the offering boxes provided.

- Notice carefully that the Bible did not say that Jesus was sitting over against the treasury making a note of WHO was giving their offering that day.

- The Bible does not say that Jesus was sitting over against the treasury looking at WHAT the people were giving.
- The Bible does not say that Jesus was sitting over against the treasury looking at WHEN the people were giving.
- The Bible does not say that Jesus was sitting over against the treasury looking at WHERE the people were coming from that were giving.
- The Bible does not say that Jesus was sitting over against the treasury looking at HOW MUCH the people were giving.

The Bible says that Jesus sat by the treasury looking at HOW, not "how much," the people were giving. In other words, Jesus was looking at the attitude and motive of the people who were giving. Please note that your purpose for doing something does not limit you from knowing other things that were not your purpose in the first place. For example, your purpose for coming to church is to worship. However, as you are worshipping, you notice there's a brother or a sister in the church today whom you have not seen in a long time. Your purpose is to worship; however, you are also aware of who is in the sanctuary with you. Jesus is concerned about our motives and attitudes toward giving. II Corinthians 9:7 says: *"Every man according as he purposed in his heart, so let him give; Not grudgingly, or of necessity: for God loveth a cheerful giver."*

The widow gave her two mites for offering despite the imperfect leadership of the temple that day. She gave her offering because of her divine responsibility and love for God. Please be mindful that those who were temple leaders at the time were the scribes and Pharisees who all were plotting to get rid of and/or kill Jesus. The scribes and Pharisees were self-righteous, egotistical men who were more concerned about how they were viewed by the people than about doing what was right, holy, and honorable before God.

- **The Benefits of Giving to the Local Church**
  As was mentioned earlier, the tithe should not be given as offerings or the offerings be given as tithe. Our churches need our offerings. This is a divine obligation for all clergies and laities. All of the financial needs that the local church has are satisfied primarily from our local giving. All of the ministries that the local church desires to provide for the church and its community are financed by our local giving. If those who return tithe would also give 3-5% of their gross income as an offering, most, if not all, of our churches would not be in any financial crisis. There are some personal benefits associated with giving an offering, as follows.

- **Giving helps us to prioritize**
  When we reflect upon some of the things we spend money on, it really shows us where our hearts are. This could include our homes, motor vehicles, elaborate wardrobes and furnishings, vacations, education, or recreational activities. We are counseled in Scripture to "lay up for yourselves treasures in heaven, where neither moth nor rust destroys, and where thieves do not break in or steal; for where our treasure is, there your heart will be also" (Matthew 6:20-21). These verses admonish us to invest money in the eternal and not only the temporal. We are encouraged to become more heavenly-minded. The Apostle Paul encourages the Believers in Colossae by telling them "to set your affection on things above and not on things on the

earth" (Colossians 3:2). Giving to the advancement of God's kingdom helps us to prioritize our lives for time and eternity. My wife and I give offerings not only to our local church but also to any ministry that we are blessed by from anywhere around the world. By doing so, we are more conscientious about how we manage the money we are blessed with so that we can be a blessing to others whom God is using to bless us.

- **Giving helps our faith to grow**

    Rightly understood, giving is not about how much money we have but how much faith we have in God to provide for and take care of us. Sometimes we pride ourselves on giving from the abundance that God has blessed us with, but I would like to challenge you as you read this book that you will also consider giving sacrificially to the kingdom of God. Sacrificial giving occurs when we give without having more or other options to turn to for replenishing what we gave. The Old Testament story found in the first book of Kings 17:9-16 comes to mind. This is the story about Elijah, the prophet's encounter with the widow of Zarephath. She only had a small morsel of meal to make herself and her son the last cake before they died. The story said that the prophet asked the widow to make him a cake first, which she sacrificially did and was blessed tremendously because of her act of kindness. Sacrificially giving is clearly a matter of trust. The widow's faith in God grew, and she believed all the word of God as it was spoken by the prophet.

- **Giving blesses us abundantly**

    The more we give unconditionally, the more God gives to us! This is not just wishful thinking or fantasy; this is true! We don't give because we want to get. We give because of our gratitude toward God for all the things (financially and otherwise) that He has given to us. We are given copious measures of blessings that include financial, physical, emotional, social, intellectual, educational, and spiritual. Jesus said that when we give, "it shall be given unto us, good measure, pressed down, and shaken together, and running over..." (Luke 6:38). We deny ourselves tremendous blessings when we are not engaged in unconditional giving to God's cause.

When I got married several years ago, one of the most refreshing experiences that my wife and I share to this day is our similarity when it comes to giving. We developed a mantra that we agreed to live as it relates to giving to friends, family, and the church. We decided that if a friend or family would ask us for a loan, we would only be willing to grant the loan or a portion of the loan that we accept that we are willing to live indefinitely without the money loaned and that it would not adversely affect our relationship with the person that the loan was made to. With regard to giving to the church, we established a system of giving to God's cause, at least what He requires of us to return to Him in obedience to the offering. My wife has consistently given at least that matching 10% with the 10% tithe every time she fills out our tithe and offerings envelope every time we receive income. We have been tremendously blessed as a result. God has increased our income several times over our marriage, blessed us with an abundance of food and clothing continuously, and there was never a bill that came to our home that we were forced to ignore because of lack of money. We continue to experience God's abundant blessings in His protection and preservation of the resources He has blessed us with.

- **There is no legitimate excuse for not giving**

    Let me again repeat this statement: God only asks us to give offerings if He first gives us an income or financial increase. We are not asked to give regardless of the situation we find ourselves in financially. We are only asked to give because God has blessed us with financial resources. One of the decisions that many church members are faced with making is, "Do I still give to my church when I am going through financial struggles?" Another question that often comes up is, "If I return my tithe faithfully, shouldn't that be enough from me to satisfy my financial obligations to God?" "Why do I have to return tithe and still give an offering when I am struggling financially?" People often try to find a legitimate excuse for not giving; however, there is no such excuse. Giving is a reflection of my obedience, faith and love for God. When I choose not to give, it is an indication that my obedience, faith, and love for God are not what they should be as a committed Christian. I have heard so many excuses for not giving offerings by church members that it would take several pages to document them. The one that I have heard most often, however, is: "If my tithe was only used for local ministries, my church would not need my offering."

Approximately 95% of the churches I visited have severe financial challenges. These challenges range from purchasing monthly supplies and paying for the utilities to expensive renovation projects and high mortgage payments. Most of our churches are consumed by these astronomically high financial obligations, which has adversely affected the primary mission of the church to evangelize the world for God. It is not surprising, therefore, that finding a solution to our financial challenges is among the most pressing needs at many of our churches.

In Seventh-day Adventist churches, the designated place or storehouse where the tithe is disbursed for the purpose of paying salaries for pastors, educators, support staff and evangelism is the local conference office. Many of our members have taken the position that the solution to their church's financial dilemma can be realized quickly if the "storehouse" is relocated to their church address. By relocating the storehouse they mean keeping both the tithe and offering collected weekly at their local church, instead of sending the tithe to a local headquarters (conference office—the designated place agreed upon by the church). While this may seem to be a solution on the surface, it would mean, for starters, that all churches would be independently operated, as opposed to the fellowship of the sisterhood of churches that we currently enjoy and appreciate. The implication of independent churches would have far-reaching negative effects and consequences. Seventh-day Adventism would no longer have a universal distinct message and identity. Let's look at three of the main reasons I have heard from church members as I travel around the northeastern area of the United States.

The main reason cited by church members why the storehouse should be relocated to their church address is: "The Conference does not give back any and sometimes not enough money to the churches." Before we discuss the notion of the Conference "giving back," let us just briefly look at what stays at the local headquarters when tithe is remitted. Only 57.75 cents from each dollar remains at the local headquarters; 42.25 cents from every dollar is used to support other ministries outside of the Northeastern Conference. The 57.75 cents from each dollar is used to pay salaries for pastors, principals, teachers, office administrative staff, campground staff, and overhead maintenance expenses, among several other important financial obligations. The local headquarters cannot give back to everyone needing assistance; it is just not financially possible.

From speaking with many stewardship leaders and church treasurers, I have discovered that the reason many of our churches are not able meet their monthly financial obligations is because of the one-third of those who return tithe consistently, still even less than a third of the church gives an offering. The treasurers believe that based on the tithe income received monthly if more members gave a bountiful offering consistently, the church would be able to satisfy its financial obligations.

The storehouse does not have to be relocated to any local church address if we all give an offering according to how God has blessed us. Let us remember that while returning our tithe to God is an act of obedience, giving a free-will bountiful offering is a demonstration of faith and love for God. My prayer is that we become so unselfish that we will be the cheerful givers God has always intended for us to be.

Is Giving Tithe and Offering Really Worship?

I grew up in church believing that the offertory was just another preliminary item during the Divine Worship service that delayed the sermon. No one seemed too excited about the offertory. When the Elder announced that it was time to collect the day's tithe and offering, I never heard anyone shout, "Praise the Lord! Hallelujah! Thank you, Jesus!" I often observed a quiet, uneasy look on the faces of some people. Or I noticed that it was the time when some people excused themselves to go to the bathroom, and some sat with their eyes closed in seemingly "deep meditation." Then, as I grew older, the offertory became a time of much more singing and less giving.

I have quoted this Bible text several times before, but allow me to reference it yet again. In spite of the most serious and solemn text in Malachi 3:8-9 — "Will a man rob God? Yet ye have robbed me. But ye say, Wherein have we robbed thee? In tithes and offerings. Ye are cursed with a curse: for ye have robbed me, even this whole nation"— many of us take the grace of God for granted. The text reminds us each week that God will hold us accountable for the monies He entrusted to us. God only requires tithe and offering from those He has given money. God has never asked us for anything (including money) that He has not provided us with in the first place.

Worship is a posture of the heart that is demonstrated in what we say and do when we come in the presence of God at any given time and place. It's our response to God for the blessings we have received from God. Worship is celebrating God and His goodness toward us. Therefore, when we return to God His tithe and give a generous free will offering, we are engaged in worship. When we worship God, we receive tremendous blessings from Him. When we deny ourselves the privilege of worshiping God with our tithe and offering, we are denying ourselves countless blessings. If we are blessed to actively participate in the worship of God during the offertory by returning God's tithe and giving a generous free will offering, then we should joyfully do so.

Let's remember that God should be treated with the utmost respect over the government of the land. This means that we should, with great gratitude, return to God His tithe from the gross amount we receive and not allow the government to be the only entity that gets money from our gross. Returning our tithe is a demonstration of our obedience to God while giving our offering is a demonstration of our love for God. According to Malachi 3:9, giving an offering is not optional but a mandate from God. Returning our tithe without giving a liberal offering still renders us robbers of God's money.

Let us continue to demonstrate our love and obedience to God by giving a liberal offering and returning His tithe. Let us look forward to worshiping the Lord in returning His tithe and generously giving Him an offering. Let's celebrate His awesome blessings of providing us with money so that we can be a blessing in helping propagate the gospel of salvation. Let us not deny ourselves this wonderful worship experience.

Thank God It's Not Another Bill

I used to try and ignore it for a long time as just semantics. "A choice of word, or just the nuances of the English language." Whenever I heard someone say that they were "paying" their tithe as opposed to saying "returning" their tithe, it is really not a big deal. However, after repeatedly hearing the phrase "I pay my tithe" at several stewardship seminars, I realized that many people do have the attitude toward returning their tithe and giving their offering as another bill they have an obligation to pay the next time they are at church.

All of us understand that we live in a society where paying bills in order to receive goods and services is necessary and important to our survival. We have necessary and important bills like mortgages, rent, insurance, taxes, food, clothing, and the list goes on indefinitely. However, I have never met anyone who has said to me that they look forward to or enjoy paying bills. We pay our bills because we have to in order to receive goods and services.

If we look at our tithe and offering as bills that we are obligated to pay when we receive income, we will not receive the intended blessings that the Lord has for those who return their tithe and offering because of love, loyalty, gratitude, and obedience. As was said earlier in this chapter, tithe, and offering are demonstrations of worship to God. We are not buying or paying for anything from God. God gives us freely all of the blessings we are in need of.

I believe that the language that we use can significantly affect our attitudes toward this sacred act of worship. I would encourage everyone reading this book to consider carefully the impact that language has on us personally and on the people that we care about deeply. The words we use are as important as the words we do not use when describing all that we do for God. Let us choose our words carefully so that our attitudes and the attitudes of others hearing us are not misguided, but they and we clearly appreciate the thoughtfulness of everything we do and say in worship to God.

Offering Is Not Optional

While most of us clergy and laity pride ourselves in returning tithe, it must be noted that giving to God only occurs when we give our offerings. The Bible is clear that we are only stewards of God's tithe. It does not belong to us, so when we return it, we are not giving from what the Lord has entrusted unto us for our domestic needs. We are simply returning to God what is rightfully His. The Bible also clearly states in Malachi 3:8 that we have a divine obligation to give our offerings to God and His tithe.

Can the Tithe Be Given as Offerings?

The question about giving our tithe as a local offering is one that is often primarily asked for three reasons:
- The church member is confused about where the storehouse is
- The church member is disregarding the difference between tithe and offering
- The church member is not pleased with the Conference administration and believes that withholding or using the tithe for other church needs is not justified

The Storehouse

As I travel around the Northeastern territory of the United States, I have been asked on many occasions to identify the storehouse that Malachi 3:10 speaks of. I have given the same response every time I have been asked. The storehouse is the church. The churches that make up the Northeastern Conference corporation, as is the case for all regional and state conferences, designate the Conference office, which is a part of the church, to be the storehouse. The tithe is returned to the storehouse and the local offerings to local churches.

The Difference Between Tithe and Offering

There is a difference between the local offerings and the tithe. A tithe is 10% of our gross income, and our offerings are our freewill gifts to God. A tithe is our obedient response to the command of God, while our offerings are a reflection of our love and loyalty to God.

Seven Reasons That Motivate Me to Give a Generous Offering

1. My offering is a reflection of my love for God.
2. My offering is used to support the local and global ministries of my church.
3. My offering is used to maintain the building that I worship God in weekly.
4. My offering is used to pay utility bills and purchase supplies for my church.
5. My offering is used to help the less fortunate in my church and community.
6. My offering is used to pay the mortgage and/or rent for the building I worship in weekly.
7. My offering is a divine requirement from God.

Takeaways from Chapter 8

(The answer to the all-important question **(How do you avoid struggling financially regardless of the amount of money you have?)**

- ☐ We should give because of our love for God
- ☐ When we give, it helps us to overcome selfishness
- ☐ Giving helps us to prioritize
- ☐ Giving helps our faith to grow in Christ
- ☐ Giving blesses us abundantly
- ☐ Giving allows God to act on our behalf
- ☐ Giving is an expression of worship
- ☐ Giving opens doors and windows of spiritual and financial blessings
- ☐ The location of the storehouse is not the issue; the selfishness of heart is what prevents us from giving

Time is one of the most important gifts God has given to us. From the time we are born until the time we die, God expects us and those who have influence over us to honor Him with the time He has given to us.

CHAPTER 9

The Big Responsibility

Sharing the Reality That Stewardship Is Not Optional

God does not bless us just to make us happy; He blesses us to make us a blessing. God requires those He has blessed financially, educationally, physically, socially, and in every way to share the benefits of being blessed with others. Our greatest responsibility as people of faith, according to Matthew 28:19-20, is to make disciples of Jesus. All of our efforts and desires as we interact with others should be to demonstrate to them in every way who Jesus is like. As a result, we need to do some internal inventory of the blessings we have received from God to determine the effectiveness of our witness of Jesus to others. We are called to evangelize the world with urgency because of the imminence of Jesus' return.

Most times, when we think of Evangelism, we think of Bible Studies, Revelation Seminars, Revivals, and Evangelistic

Crusades. While these forms of Evangelistic outreach are amongst some of the most popular ways used by most churches, there are several other ways that have proven to be effective methods to share Jesus with others.

One of the most effective forms of Evangelism that I have experienced is simply sharing my personal experiences of Jesus with others in an informal, relaxed atmosphere. I have also discovered that the most impactful things I have shared with others that inspired them to be interested in wanting to hear more about Jesus are the things that address immediate needs. Many people with whom I have shared my experiences about my relationship with Jesus found at least one of two stewardship principles fascinating. These are time management and money management. They wanted to hear more because these two interrelated principles are the concerns of most people in our society today.

Stewardship Evangelism of Time

Everything we do, we utilize this principle of time. It takes time to do everything: planning, organizing and executing ideas. Despite our best efforts, many people often report that they just don't have enough time to do the things they would like to do. Since it seems like we never have enough time to do the many things we would like to do, wisely managing our time is extremely important.

The issue of time management is something we all have to navigate effectively in order to get the best results for ourselves. God is the creator of time, and as such, he is the greatest resource we can go to in order to learn how we can become effective in time management. When God created the seven days of the week in the account found in Genesis 1, He created time. The very first verse in Genesis 1:1, which says, *"In the beginning, God created the heaven and the earth,"* speaks directly to the first recorded time in the history of heaven and earth. The "beginning" is the time that it happened. The "beginning" is the time that God, who transcends time, created time for humanity to govern ourselves with. Every time we read the phrase, "And the evening and the morning were the first, second, third…day." God was in those moments dividing time, using day and night as demarcations. God did something specific on each day, or for each period of time, to illustrate to us how we should go about managing the time He has given to us. He could have done everything that He did in one or two days, but God divided time into seven days, with the seventh day as a rest from all the activities that He performed to give us parameters of how we should do the things that we are required to do. It is important to note that if rest time is not incorporated into our plans for any extended period of time, we will ruin ourselves.

Time of Work

From the beginning of creation, we are introduced to work by God. The first verse of the Bible says, "In the beginning God created…" God created or performed work at the inception of time. God worked for six consecutive days before creating a day for rest. On the sixth day when God decided to create human beings, the Bible informs us in Genesis 1:26 (KJV), *"And God said, let us make man in our image, after our likeness: and let them have dominion over the fish of the sea, and over the fowl of the air, and over the cattle, and over all the earth, and over every creeping thing that crept upon the earth."* To have dominion over all the animals and over all the earth means that man was created to have control over everything that God created upon the earth. To exercise this control means that humanity had the right to do what was in the best interest of the animals and the earth. This control or dominion would necessitate work. Genesis 2:15 (KJV) says, *"And the Lord God took the man and put him into the garden of Eden to dress it and to keep it."* To "dress it and to keep it" means to take care of it and to look after it. This implies that God gave humanity the responsibility to spend time working to look after and care for the garden.

Please note that work was introduced to humanity before sin interrupted the relationship they had with God. Spending time to work is, therefore, not a result of sin but a result of being created. As good stewards, we have a responsibility to share with humanity this God-given responsibility that time should be invested to work. In counseling the church at Thessalonica, the Apostle Paul says in 2 Thessalonians 3:10 (KJV), "...if any *(man)* would not work, neither should he eat." Spending time working is synonymous with living. A person who is able to, but refuses to, work is not deserving of life.

We have a great responsibility as stewards to remind everyone of the salient truth of spending time to work. The ability to work is a God-given blessing and responsibility that we should treat with the utmost respect and gratitude. We are able to live independent and productive lives when we use our abilities to perform work that God has gifted us to do. When we refuse to spend time working, we are not only denying ourselves copious blessings, but we are also denying those whom God intended to bless by our efforts.

We are expected to spend time engaging in physical and mental work. The physical work that we are engaged in each day may not necessarily mean work that is performed for the primary source of income for sustenance. Physical work is important for improving our overall health and the well-being of others. Spending time engaged in physical work builds community and fosters relationships that otherwise may not have been realized. Mental work refers primarily to work performed by the brain and the mind. It is also of vital importance that we spend time engaging our minds with stimulants that will shape our thoughts and actions for our good and the good of others. God has given humanity wisdom and abilities that are second to none. When we spend time developing our minds through spiritual and social interactions and meaningful relationships, we are positioning ourselves for unlimited possibilities in impacting the world around us.

Along with the time we use for physical and mental work, the time invested in spiritual work is of great value. Spiritual work is anything we do to help ourselves and others to deepen our relationship with God. This may include time spent in Bible study, praying and fasting, worship and meditation services, witnessing about who God is, and sharing His love with others. God expects us as good stewards to be engaged in well-meaning time and effort in maintaining and helping others to become more intimately connected to Him.

Time of Rest

The time created to rest each week, known as the Sabbath day, is invaluable to all of humanity. God created us with the innate need for this special time of rest every week. Our bodies are able to do and undergo tremendous stress for a certain period of time, but if stretched beyond their limit will break down dramatically. A time of physical rest is important for replenishing the body, mind, and spirit. This important time facilitates the reduction of stress, lowers and maintains blood pressure, and provides a variety of health benefits for all the organs of the body. A time of physical rest also aids in healing the body from any kind of physical injury that it sustains. Our bodies were created with the ability to perform extreme feats for short periods before needing rest. To ignore this cycle is to push the body beyond its capacity to do what it was created for well. As good stewards of time, we have a responsibility to maintain and educate our fellow humans on the importance of managing the time for rest.

In addition to the overwhelming importance of time for physical rest, we also have a responsibility to share with others the need for time for mental rest. The rest intervals that our bodies need at the intervals of each day and week for Sabbath rest are also designed to provide us with mental rest. Mental rest is giving the brain and mind a break from the constant processes of analyzing information that is being poured into it. It gives the brain some quiet time from the activities of work and caring for self and others. This break time for the brain will promote greater joy and happiness, as well as reduce stress and anxiety. It will help us to concentrate better when we go back to using our minds again after a mental break. Our memory and immune systems will be improved as a result of the time taken for our mental health care needs. I have discovered that I am able to do more work effectively after giving my brain a break from the constant chatter of noise and information that I am processing. I am able to share the thoughts that God has placed in my mind for this book early in the mornings after a good night's rest. I have tried writing at the end of a busy day or just before retiring for bed but have found that those times are not the best for my mental capacity to function at its best. Again, here is another reason for the responsibility to share with our fellow human family the importance of managing our time well to achieve optimum mental health care. God created us with the need to manage time well so that we can enjoy the best that He offers us in life. The effective management of the time we have been given is also designed to prepare us for eternity; that is, time without end.

This brings me to one of the most important responsibilities for having to share the importance of good time management, and that is it promotes spiritual rest. Spiritual rest is simply time with God. Time with God and not necessarily time doing things for God. We can become tired, worn out, and burnt out from doing things for God, but we will never be exhausted from spending time with God. The results of spending time with God for rejuvenation and revitalization are to prepare us for living and doing the things of God. At the end of the creation week, God created the Sabbath, a special time of rest to commune with humanity without the distraction of work and other social responsibilities that He entrusted to mankind. God's desire for Sabbath rest is to allow us the opportunity to deepen and come into closer intimacy in our relationship with Him. This is the most crucial of all our time management responsibilities. One of the most profound and sobering Bible verses in the New Testament that speaks to time management is Mark 8:36 (KJV), which says, *"What shall it profit a man if he shall gain the whole world, and lose his own soul?"* In other words, if I spend all my time accomplishing all the wonderful things that life offers, but I am still lost, then my time on earth would have been in vain! The time of spiritual rest that we are commanded to have on Sabbaths, as well as the shorter intervals of time during the six days before the Sabbath, is invaluable to us having a saving relationship with God. To be good stewards of time means that we have an awesome responsibility to share with everyone the extreme importance of time for spiritual rest!

Stewardship Evangelism and Money

The Bible has a lot to say about money. Jesus, His disciples, and the Apostle Paul spent more time teaching about money than they did teaching about faith and prayer combined.

Why would Jesus spend so much of His time teaching about money? Maybe Jesus understands the significant impact that money would have on our relationship with God. Could it be that Jesus knew that just before His second coming, one of the things that would be our greatest desire is the accumulation of money? Or maybe Jesus knew there would be a great disparity between the rich and the poor, so He wanted to underscore that people should not be treated based on their economic standing but rather based on their love for God and their love for their fellow men. One thing is certain, and that is money is a very interesting, important, and intriguing subject that appeals to many.

Since one of the things that most, if not all, of us have in common is our need for money, people are always interested in hearing how they can get more money or how they can get more from their money. One of the most intriguing discussions I have had with people about money management is their ability to give despite their individual need for money. It sounds almost oxymoronic that one should be engaged in giving money when they also have a need for money themselves. Yet, giving money is one of the guaranteed ways of receiving money, according to Scripture. Many financial experts also agree with the Bible that giving and investing are two ways to increase income. While it is true that money is very important to us to obtain goods and services, it is also true that money has some limitations in addressing some of life's greatest challenges. Money is not always able to provide lasting happiness and joy. There are just some things that money can and cannot do.

Is Money the Answer?

Have you ever read the Bible verse found in Ecclesiastes 10:19, which says, "...money is the answer for everything"? If you have, what was your initial response? If you have never read this verse written by the wise man Solomon and you are hearing it for the first time, what is your immediate reaction? Is your reaction, "Is it really?" or "That cannot be true!" or maybe, "If the Bible says it, then oh well." When it comes to the subject of money, there are so many theories, teachings, perspectives, and even doctrines. What is the truth about money? What do we really believe as Christians?

Before we look closer at this text in Ecclesiastes 10:19, we have heard it said that "money cannot buy happiness!" Yet, it is true that many people are sad even as they read this brief article about money because they do not have the money they would like to address their financial obligations. For many people, money is indeed the answer for everything, or at least, that's what they often think.

In order for us to understand what the Bible is saying here in Ecclesiastes 10:19, we have to closely examine the context of the scripture and not just go away saying what the Bible says, but rather, go away saying what the Bible teaches. What the Bible says, if not properly understood based on its context to identify what the Bible is teaching, can lead to grave errors. It is helpful for us to read the preceding verses beginning at verse 16 to understand the content clearly. The (KJV) reads as follows:

"Woe to you, O land, when your king is a child, and our princes feast in the morning! Blessed are you, O land, when your king is the son of nobles, and your princes feast at the proper time—for strength and not for drunkenness! Because of laziness the building decays and through idleness of hands the house leaks. A feast is made for laughter, and wine makes merry; but money answers everything."

The distinction between an honorable and a dishonorable king in verses 16-18 is clear; a country with an honorable king who governs with sobriety and strength is blessed, but the country with a lazy and drunken king will come to ruin.

In verse 19, we are shown the attitude of the drunken king (one who lives for pleasure and becomes drunk with wine) and for whom MONEY will provide everything they need to continue their life of pleasure and partying. It is clear, therefore, that Solomon is not expressing his personal position on the benefits of money, but rather he is highlighting his observations of the lazy, pleasure-seeking kings around him. A good example of this kind of king was Belshazzar, King of Babylon.

Money is a gift from God. It must be managed well and given its appropriate priority in our lives, which reflects that it is used to give glory to God in all of its usages. James W. Frick says it this way: "Don't tell me where your priorities are. Show me where you spend your money, and I'll tell you what they are." For the self-seeking, self-absorbed individual with a horizontal vision on the things of this world: money is the answer for everything. However, for the individual seeking righteousness with a vertical vision of things above: godly money management is the principle that all of us need to govern ourselves with.

Once I was audited by the Internal Revenue Service (IRS). The auditor explained that the reason I was being audited was that there was one particular concern that had been reoccurring for several years with the tax documents that I filed. The concern was the amount of money that I gave annually as a charitable contribution to my church in tithe and offering. This gave me an opportunity to share with the IRS auditor my religious and spiritual beliefs regarding tithe and offering. The auditor shared that he did not know that tithe was a spiritual obligation to God. He further stated that he thought it was optional. I took the opportunity to share the purpose of returning tithe as a demonstration of my obedience to God and my offerings as a demonstration of my love and gratitude to God. People often find it amazing that pastors also return tithe and give a generous freewill offering.

I have a friend who thinks that people who return tithe and give offerings have been brainwashed by their pastors. He said he could not understand in a world where there are so many people who are working hard to survive, that those people would be willing to give so much money to the church.

After sharing with him several money management principles and the reasons for giving, he became interested in learning more about giving tithe and offering. He reported that the principle of giving has helped him to overcome many of his selfish tendencies. He told me that since he began practicing better money management principles, including giving money away to various charities, he has been receiving a lot more non-salary income. I told him it is quite common for people who are engaged in cheerful giving to experience increased financial blessings from God. As a result of that experience, he is more interested in knowing more about my church and my beliefs in God.

Money Can Be a Blessing and Curse

God's intention is that money will be a blessing to all those who receive it. However, if not managed as God intends for it to be, it can be a vicious and deadly curse. Here are some ways that money can be a tremendous blessing when managed according to God's precepts and examples:

- Money can be an invitation to experience great blessing by being a blessing. Generosity allows us to respond to others' physical needs and, as we do, to participate in

activities that are literally of eternal consequence (see Acts 20:35; Malachi 3:10).
- Money can be used to propagate the gospel around the world. This will help those who are in the darkness of sin to experience the bright light of salvation.
- Money can provide us with the freedom to choose what, when, where, who and how we want to live socially. This does not mean that we will achieve perfection, but that we can avoid or reduce certain ills of society.
- Money can provide us with opportunities to pursue our dreams, goals, and ambitions. With good management of money, we are able to launch out into the deep of our imaginations and aspirations that we would otherwise be limited to if we did not have the financial resources available.
- Money can provide us with security to have some of life's basic needs without much concern. Food, shelter, clothing, and safety are obtainable when we have money at our disposal.
- Money can aid in one becoming content. Financial contentment does not require a specific sum of money. It is being satisfied with having some money and using it to invest and/or spend on the things that bring happiness and joy to a person's heart.

Money, if not managed by spiritual principles, can also be spiritually dangerous! Here are four reasons why money can be a curse:

- Money can blur your spiritual vision and cause you to forget God. Having financial needs inspires us to call upon God and maintain an intimate relationship with

Him. Physical needs draw us close to God. When our basic physical needs are satisfied, we sometimes do not see the need to draw as close to God as when we have severe needs. It's hard for them to think of themselves as spiritually destitute.
- Money can cause us to think about ourselves with pride and pompousness and can cause us to look down on others. While we ought to be thankful for the amount of money we are blessed with, that does not give us the license to look down and degrade others who do not have the amount of money we have.
- Money can weaken your resolve to be law-abiding and people of integrity. Money can be dangerous because it removes a restraint—affordability. Most of us can't afford to pursue every desire that pops into our hearts. It's typically not because we have such a strong commitment to fight temptation and choose instead to live for the Kingdom of God.
- Those who desire to be rich fall into temptation, into a snare, into many senseless and harmful desires that plunge people into ruin and destruction (1 Timothy 6:9).
- Money can finance your allegiance to the kingdom of self. There is no neutrality when it comes to your finances; what you are doing is worship. I have rarely misused money because I was ignorant or without a budget. No, I dishonored the Lord with my wallet because, at that particular moment, I didn't care what God or anyone else said. I wanted what I wanted, and if I had the resources to chase it, I did.
- No one can serve two masters, for either he will hate the one and love the other, or he will be devoted to the one and despise the other. You cannot serve God and money (Matthew 6:24).

Now, it must be stated that there is no teaching in Scripture that would lead us to believe that poor people are better off spiritually than others. The Bible also emphasizes the tremendous good that can be done with accumulated wealth.

But in our daily experience with money, the Word of God alerts us to the many dangers that it poses. Our only defense is the powerful grace of the Redeemer. He comes and lives inside of us so that when desire within meets temptation without, we will have just what we need to fight the battle.

Stewardship of Environment

Soon after the creation of mankind, God gave humans the responsibility to take care of the earth. Genesis 2:15 (KJV) says, *"And the Lord God took the man, and put him into the garden of Eden to dress it and to keep it."* In other words, the first assignment that humanity was tasked with was to be good stewards of the environment that God created for them to live in and be a part of. As stewards, Adam and Eve had the divine responsibility to take care of the earth. They were expected to ensure that the plants, animals, land, and water were treated with great care and respect. They understood that they were not owners of the earth and its inhabitants, but stewards of it. Psalms 24:1 (KJV) says that "the earth is the Lord's and the fullness thereof; the world, and they that dwell therein." How we treat the earth and its inhabitants, is a reflection of our commitment to adhere to the divine mandate to be good stewards of our environment. God does not excuse us from this responsibility because of any reason or circumstances at any time. This means that despite the fact that we may be great proponents of certain doctrinal beliefs that are dear to us, like the second coming, the state of the dead, or the Sabbath, these doctrines do not negate the importance of the doctrine of the environment.

Since being a good steward of the environment is a spiritual requirement from God, we have the responsibility of sharing this most important truth with everyone we come in contact with. The sharing of this truth should not be designed only to protect the interest of the environment or for civic pride but, most importantly, to point people to the God that created the environment. Everything that God has entrusted unto us as stewards should be managed in a manner that points people to Him. Sharing with people the gospel of Jesus Christ through the lens of the environment may be more effective in some cases than some of the more traditional Bible studies and church services approaches in winning souls for the kingdom of God. It is important that in our efforts to evangelize the world, we are intentional in researching topics and issues that are pertinent to the needs of those we are trying to reach with the gospel. Identifying mutual areas of concern and interest with those we are endeavoring to reach with the gospel of Jesus will help us to have an opening wedge that others who are well-intentioned with traditional approaches may not have similar success with having an audience with some individuals.

I had the privilege of meeting and working with a lady who is passionate about environmental awareness evangelism. Her name is Natalie Patasaw. She is an adjunct professor at the State University of New York. She teaches various courses related to the environment and is also passionately involved in her community, where she serves as chairperson of the Rockland County Environmental Management Council. She shared the following experience she had a few years ago with her church family:

> Everywhere people turn, there is more discussion and news coverage about environmental concerns.

From the 200 Native American nations represented at the Standing Rock Reservation pipeline protest in North Dakota to people recycling things at home, we are more aware of protecting God's creation now than ever before.

Lately, two churches in the Rockland County area have included a segment in their worship services to spotlight environmental awareness. The pastors and church members began noticing that their surrounding communities were becoming increasingly aware of the importance of protecting the local environment. The challenge for these local congregations was to tap into their communities based on the concerns of the communities and not what the churches wanted to conveniently offer from their traditional arsenal of church programs.

One of the churches established an Environmental Awareness Evangelism project. This project was designed with a multifaceted approach to connect the church with the community. The project included:

- Two flash-mob, street concerts
- Cleaning up a neighborhood park
- An essay contest for elementary and junior high school students
- A scholarship for graduating high school students intending to pursue a major in environmental science
- A movie night and discussion on environmental issues
- A spoken Word Performance to coincide with Earth Day activities.

These activities created a stronger relationship between the churches and their communities. The churches are now able to more effectively reach their communities with the gospel of Jesus Christ because they were able to address the environmental need that both the churches and communities valued as important.

Since our first encounter with God is through creation, it is important that we allow God's creative power and presence to reveal His true identity. We allow this to happen when we take care of God's creation of the earth. When we allow the beauty and the splendor of God's creation to speak to us, we get a glimpse into the character of God. The Psalmist David says in Psalms 19:1-2 (KJV), *"The heavens declare the glory of God; and the firmament sheweth his handy work. Day unto day uttereth speech, and night unto night sheweth knowledge."* The atmospheric heavens keep telling of the wonders of God, and the skies declare the wonderful things he has done. Each day informs us of the following day, and each night announces the arrival of another night. When we are good stewards of God's environment we are testifying of God's love for us.

When we are good stewards of our environment, we are promoting a healthier living place for us to live in. The more we take care of the environment, and share with each other the importance of doing so, the better it will be for us living right now and those who will inhabit the earth in the future. Air and water pollutants are harmful to our health and put the most vulnerable in our society at increasing risk for severe health issues and/or death. When air and water are polluted, we are not only putting ourselves at risk but also the plants and animals around us. As stewards of our environment, we have a responsibility to share such vital truth with everyone we come in contact with; failure to do so is to participate in the suicidal process of innocent victims.

It is of extreme importance that we share the message of environmental stewardship with everyone, as people sometimes are unaware of the things they are doing that might be contributing to their own ruin environmentally. While nature provides us with some of the best natural raw materials needed to satisfy our basic needs, it is important for us to manage how much and how often we take from nature to satisfy these needs. We need wood to provide lumber for the construction of buildings, furniture, and other equipment. However, deforestation can result in soil erosion and the misplacement of wildlife to spread over into urban areas where people will have difficulty living with displaced animals. It is also important for us to be good stewards of marine life and the drinking water supply. Recreational activities on water may be entertaining and provide for a good family time together; however, the equipment used to perform these activities may be detrimental to marine life. The use of chemicals too close to drinking water and other domestic usages of water supply can be a high health risk issue for other human beings to live with. These are only some of the many reasons we need to share the message of being good stewards of our environment.

Takeaways from Chapter 9

(The answer to the all-important question **(How do you avoid struggling financially regardless of the amount of money you have?)**

☐ God does not bless us just to make us happy; He blesses us to make us a blessing.

☐ The issue of time management is something that everyone has to effectively navigate in order to get the best results for themselves. God is the creator of time, and as such, he is the greatest resource we can go to in order to learn how we can become effective in time management.

☐ We have a great responsibility as stewards to remind everyone of the salient truth of spending time to work. The ability to work is a God-given blessing and responsibility that we should treat with the utmost respect and gratitude. We are able to live independent and productive lives when we use our abilities to perform work that God has gifted us to do.

☐ The time created to rest each week, known as the Sabbath day, is invaluable to all of humanity. God created us with the innate need for this special time of rest every week. Our bodies are able to do and undergo tremendous stress for a certain period of time, but if stretched beyond their limit will break down dramatically.

- ☐ While it is true that money is very important to us to obtain goods and services, it is also true that money has some limitations in addressing some of life's greatest challenges. Money is not always able to provide lasting happiness and joy. There are just some things that money can and cannot do.

- ☐ Since being a good steward of the environment is a spiritual requirement from God, we have the responsibility of sharing this most important truth with everyone we come in contact with. The sharing of this truth should not be designed only to protect the interest of the environment or for civic pride but, most importantly, to point people to the God that created the environment.

CHAPTER 10

The Big Blessing

What Does Stewardship Have to Do with Salvation?

When it is all said and done, how will it end? After all of the seminars, Bible studies, sermons, and religious programs and events come to an end, what's next? For most Bible-believing Christians, it is the long-awaited return of Jesus Christ to earth for the sole purpose of taking those who were sincere Believers before their deaths and those who are still alive and are in an intimate relationship with Him. The primary goal of Christianity is to be saved when Jesus comes back to earth at the end of the world as we know it today. Therefore, all the spiritual and religious practices that we are engaged in should prepare us for this great climactic event that I believe will take place someday soon. If being a good steward of the resources God has entrusted to us does not prepare us for this special transformative event, then it should not be one of the spiritual disciplines that we are asked to live by. In other words, if it is not of utmost importance to our salvation at the second coming of Jesus, it should not be emphasized as such. However, if it is not an optional religious discipline but rather evidence of a committed relationship with God, then it ought to be taught, understood and practiced as such.

Rightly understood, it is impossible to be saved without being a good steward of all the resources that God lavishly has bestowed upon us. We have already established several times throughout this book that those who steal from God His tithe and offering, and refuse to repent and return unto God what is rightfully His, will not be numbered amongst the saved at the second coming of Jesus! How we manage our finances will determine if we will be amongst the saved or the lost when Jesus comes. It is as important as that! Anything that is so important cannot be optional! Therefore, being good stewards is as important to being saved when Jesus returns to earth as obeying all of God's commandments is to be in a saving relationship with God.

We often look at stewardship through a very narrow lens of returning tithe and giving a liberal freewill offering. However, we know that stewardship is far more encompassing than that. As we have said repeatedly throughout this book, Christian stewardship is managing God's resources, God's way, for God's glory. Therefore, being a Christian steward means that I have a divine obligation to God to manage all the things He has entrusted to me in a manner that brings honor and glory to His name. The realization that I am being held accountable by God is an awesome responsibility that I should not take lightly. Whatever God has given to me, I should show my appreciation by being a good steward of His blessings.

For Christians, the second coming means the final act performed by Jesus to save all Believers from sin. It is, therefore, the most precious promise that God has given to us. The second coming is a gift for all those who have accepted the gift of salvation offered to us by Jesus. Salvation is far more important than money. While money can give us many temporary opportunities, it is limited in providing us with eternal satisfaction. The gift of salvation is the most amazing gift that we have been asked to be good stewards of. Let me be clear here as I speak about salvation. I am not talking about a religious concept or an event in the future, but rather I am speaking of Jesus as the embodiment of our salvation. As we look at the subject of stewardship and salvation, we are indeed looking at what it means to have an intimate relationship with Jesus and be ready for His second coming.

The direct question that needs to be asked is: can someone be saved and not be a good steward at the second coming of Jesus? The most direct answer is an emphatic No! To be saved means to be obedient to the Word of God as a result of allowing the Holy Spirit's power to control our lives. To be saved means to accept by faith the death and resurrection of Jesus Christ as the ultimate price for our sins. To be a good steward of salvation means that I allow the Holy Spirit to guide me into making decisions that reflect my love and commitment to Jesus for saving me. It means how much time I spend in prayer, Bible study, and sharing Jesus with others. It further means my life reflects that I am ready to meet Jesus at His second coming.

As a good steward of the salvation that I have received from God, my responsibility is to demonstrate in all areas of my life that I am blessed with the gift of salvation. This should be easily seen in my stewardship of the other gifts I received from God. How I manage the time that I am entrusted with each day should reflect that the gift of salvation is the most important thing to me. At the end of each day, it should be seen that most of the time spent or invested was time that helped me and those that I spent it with to appreciate the gift of salvation.

The same should be true with how I use the talents God has entrusted unto me. First, I ought to acknowledge that my talents are good gifts from God. These talents are given to me to be used to glorify God as an expression of my appreciation to God for the salvation He has given me. I glorify God with my talents by using them to help others come to a saving knowledge of the salvation Jesus offers to all mankind. If my talents include music, then I should ask God to help me use my musical talent to testify of His saving grace. Whatever my talents are, they should be used to honor God based on my love and acceptance of the gift of salvation that He has blessed me with.

Stewardship is, therefore, the Christian's appropriate response to the precious gift of salvation given by God for our benefit. We cannot be saved and not be good stewards of God's blessings. Being a good steward is a natural response to God for all of His blessings. We are happy to be good stewards of God's many blessings to demonstrate to God how grateful we are for being entrusted with His blessings. We are looking forward to the second coming of Jesus with joyful expectations because, by the aid of the Holy Spirit, we have learned to be good stewards of all of His blessings.

Stewardship During a Pandemic

The message and meaning of who is a good steward of the resources God has blessed us with are seen most clearly during a pandemic. During the uncertainties of a pandemic, every one of us is confronted with making crucial decisions about the resources that are available to us. These decisions often reflect what our main priorities are in life. These priorities will be determined by the things we deem most important and valuable to us. Those of us who honor God with our tithe, offering, time, talent, and gifts during a pandemic do so because of the priority that God has in our lives. We choose to remain good and faithful stewards because we believe that it is the very least we can do to show our God our most sincere gratitude to Him for who He is in our lives.

During the heights of the Coronavirus pandemic of the year 2020, with all of the uncertainties of the effects that it would have on society, I discovered that most of the churches that make up the constituency that I am a member of continued to experience consistent financial support. Many analysts and financial experts predicted that we would experience a significant decrease of 25-40 percent in tithe income to our churches. This expected decrease would result in layoffs, significant budget cuts in funding ministries, and minimal resources available to assist members of our community. However, the decrease that most churches experienced was less than 20 percent. Some churches experienced an increase in tithe and others saw tithe income from members who were very delinquent and inconsistent with returning tithe.

Whatever may have been the personal motivation behind the increases in tithe during the pandemic, I do not know. One thing I heard consistently from the pastors and laity that I spoke with was people want to be ready to meet Jesus in the right relationship when He comes back. People associate being a good steward of their finances with a spiritual obligation that helps in preparation for eternal life. This sentiment is indeed true; only good stewards will be able to return with Jesus to heaven when he comes back for the faithful from all ages.

The Role of Good Stewards Before the Second Coming of Jesus

Good stewards are important in helping to prepare themselves and others for the second coming of Jesus. These are individuals who are consistently looking at the resources God has entrusted to them and are looking for opportunities to use these resources to help others. The Apostle Paul reminds us in his letter to the Philippian church that their generosity as good stewards provided him with the opportunity to reach others with the gospel of Jesus.

In his letter, the Apostle Paul encouraged the Philippian church members to remain encouraged in the Lord regardless of the obstacles that the devil would place before them. He asked that they remember that they belong to the Lord, and as such, they should work together harmoniously as they prepare for the Lord's second coming. He continues to share with them just how thankful he is to God for their financial generosity in helping him to reach others with the gospel, and he added that he was confident that God would bless them, therefore, in the same manner, that they had been a blessing to him. Paul reminds the Philippian church that "God shall supply all their needs according to His riches in glory by Christ Jesus." In other words, Paul was affirming to the Philippian church that God would provide for their needs, in the same way God used them to provide for his needs. This is a very important reminder for all of us good stewards. God will satisfy all the needs of those who are partnering with Him to prepare people for the second coming of Jesus. This is good news for all of us who have so many outstanding needs that desperately need to be addressed.

Another very important role that we have as good stewards is to help others overcome the spirit of selfishness. As we prepare for the second coming of Jesus, we are endeavoring to become unselfish in all areas of our lives. Selfishness in any area is sin in some areas, and sin in some areas will prevent us from returning to heaven with Jesus at His second coming. Therefore, being a good steward means that we ought to demonstrate generosity in all areas of our lives. All of us can be more generous with the varied resources that God has given to us. We can give more of our time to help others learn more about Jesus and become more like him. We can give more of our financial resources to aid in the spreading of the gospel of Jesus Christ. Whatever the resource may be, God is inviting us to share it with others abundantly to demonstrate unselfishness and love for others to be saved. With the unselfishness that Jesus demonstrated in leaving the splendor of heaven to come down to earth to generously give of Himself for us to be saved, we are encouraged to unselfishly share all that we have with others so that they can be ready to meet Jesus at His second coming ready to return to heaven with Him.

Takeaways from Chapter 10

(The answer to the all-important question **(How do you avoid struggling financially regardless of the amount of money you have?)**

- ☐ The second coming of Jesus is the next great event that will happen soon. Stewardship helps us to prepare for this event.

- ☐ Being a good steward helps others to hear about and become like Jesus.

- ☐ Good stewards help others to overcome selfishness in their lives.

- ☐ Being a good steward is not relegated only to good times. Good stewards remain good because even though their situations may change, their God will never change.

- ☐ Being a good steward is as important as any other spiritual discipline that God requires of us to practice prior to the second coming of Jesus.

- ☐ As a good steward of the salvation that I have received from God, my responsibility is to demonstrate in all areas of my life that I am blessed with the gift of salvation.

CHAPTER 11

The Big Picture

What Does This Really Mean in the Grand Scheme of Things?

I read an intriguing story some time ago. The story began with a quote from Abraham Lincoln, who said: "If I had six hours to chop down a tree, I'd spend the first four hours sharpening the axe." What did he mean? The story continues:

> A young man approached the foreman of a logging crew and asked for a job. "Let's see you fell this tree first," said the foreman. The young man stepped forward and skillfully felled the large tree. The foreman was very impressed and said to the young man: "You can start on Monday." Monday, Tuesday, Wednesday came and went. On Thursday afternoon the foreman came to the young man and said: "You can pick up your paycheck on your way out today."

Startled, the young man exclaimed, "But I thought you paid on Friday!"

"That's right," said the foreman, "but I am letting you go today because you have fallen behind. Our daily felling charts show that you have dropped from first place on Monday to last place today."

"But I work really hard," said the young man. "I arrive early, I leave late, and I even work through my breaks. Please don't just fire me."

The foreman knew this to be true, and sensing the young man's integrity, stopped and thought for a bit. Then he asked: "Have you been sharpening your axe?"

The young man replied: "No sir. I have been working too hard to take time for that."[11]

The big picture when it comes to felling trees is that you need a sharpened axe. You can have an axe, have the physical strength required to fell a tree, but if you have a dull axe you will not get the job done in a timely manner.

Having shared with you so many principles about stewardship, what really is the big picture that I would like you to take away from reading this book? Here it is: stewardship is really about trust. We are willing to be good stewards if we trust the owner. This is it! I am sorry if I disappoint you. I don't know if you were expecting something that sounds more profound and scholarly, but at the deepest root of stewardship the big picture we need to examine closely is trust.

---

11   https://www.datainsighttraining.com/blog/a-lesson-from-a-very-wise-man

What is so fascinating about trust and being a good steward?

Good relationships are based on trust. In order to have a meaningful relationship with anyone or anything, there must be an element of trust. Trust is simply having a firm belief in a person or thing. In order for trust to develop, time must be invested in getting to know the person or thing. There is not a special time-formula that I can recommend to you that will satisfy every relationship. The time it will take for you to trust someone or something completely depends on how important the thing or person is to you. So let me repeat this basic truth that is fundamental to long-lasting, productive relationships: in order to know something or someone well enough to exercise trust we must be willing to invest as much time as is required. The challenge that exists in many relationships, including the one we have with God, is that people are often not willing to invest the time necessary to forge a relationship of trust that matters. We have transactional relationships that satisfy each other conveniently, but as soon as someone or one part is not able to transactionally satisfy a need when required, the relationship falls apart.

We truly trust what and who we believe we really know! The reality is that the main reason so many people struggle with being a good steward of the money, for example, that God entrusted them with is that they know money more than they know God. They have taken the time necessary to get to know what money can do. They know the influence of money and the allure that money provides. They have seen the impact money has on people. Therefore, they believe that the answer and/or solution to their problems can be satisfied by money. Having such confidence in the importance and value of money, they make their decisions based on how much money they have and not on God who provided them with the money. This is because they don't know what God is able to do, because they have not yet known God in a manner in which they can trust Him to provide for them despite the amount of money they have. They do not believe they can do what He has asked them to do if financially and logically it just doesn't make sense.

When we trust God, our attitude toward God will be reflected in our stewardship of all that He has given to us. We will relate to God in a loving, grateful and submissive manner because we recognize Him as the true source of all that we have been blessed with. When we are truly in a trusting relationship with God, we will live less stressful lives because we are confident He knows the things we are in need of and He will not withhold any good gifts from us (Psalms 84:11). When we are in a trusting relationship with God we will live joyful and happier lives because we are dependent not on the things God has provided us with for happiness and joy, but rather on knowing that we serve a God that cares for us and always desires the best for us. This means that we believe all of our needs and obligations, regardless of how severe they might be, are not going to be matters of anxiety and worry because we trust God. This does not mean that we do not use the ability God has given us to work to earn an income, live within our means and make wise decisions. This means that we are going to trust God in all areas of our lives so we do not unnecessarily place ourselves in presumptuous situations and say we are trusting God to come through for us.

Trusting God means that I am willing to allow God to direct my life in all areas. We cannot compartmentalize our lives and relationship with God. We must be willing to trust God with our health, wealth, food, family, job and everything else He has blessed us with. Many people, when they get sick, profess to trust that God can and will heal them. However, they do not trust God to follow His principles of health and well-being that would prevent them from becoming sick in the first place. There are others who are willing to trust God with their health in both preventative and restorative manners, but they do not trust God with the wealth He provides them with. They believe it is their right to use the money they have been given to do what they want to do regardless of how God said they should manage it. Yet, when they are in need of money to satisfy their needs, they believe they can turn on the "trust button" and believe that God should provide them with the money they need. Trusting God is not a desire for God to give us the things we want to satisfy our temporal needs, regardless of how we manage the things if we should get them. Trusting God is believing that God's instructions for my life are what's best for me and I am willing to live my life in accordance with His divine purpose and plan.

I once heard a report during the 1988 Winter Olympics about blind skiers training for the Olympics. Skiing can be a dangerous sporting activity even for the most skilled sighted athletes, but for blind athletes this risk is even more precarious. The report sounded like this:

> Prior to the 1988 Olympics, there was a television show about training blind skiers in slalom racing. Trainees would start off using a flat area and would be paired with a sighted skier. The blind skiers learned to turn right and left and were then taken to the slalom slopes. Sighted skiers would ski with them and shout, "Left!" "Right!" "Right!" The trainees would turn when their sighted partner told them. They relied solely on the word of their sighted partner. If they relied on that word and turned when they were told to turn, then everything would turn

out perfect. It was either trust or catastrophe! By listening to that sighted partner, they would finish the course and get across the finish line.[12]

This is what it means to trust in the word of God. We do what the word of God says in complete trust and obedience, or suffer great catastrophe if we do not heed it. If we take God at His Word, He will help us to safely navigate the course of life despite the dangers seen or unseen and bring us to the finish line. We must trust in the word of God unconditionally! God's words are a transcript of His character and can be trusted to guide our lives in the direction that is best for us.

Exercising complete trust in God is the essence of what it means to be a good steward. This means that regardless of the amount of resources we have at our disposal, we will always turn to God for instruction and direction and never away from Him. Even if logically it doesn't seem to make any sense to you or others, you have decided that come what may, you will always turn to God whether your situation changes or not. It's easier to turn to God when our resources are diminishing, but it is sometimes much harder to turn to God when our situation has bottomed out. This means not when things are getting bad, but when things are at their worst. In order for us to put our trust in God when we have more bills than money, we must practice putting our trust in Him when we have more money than bills. I can hear somebody reading the previous sentence and saying to themselves, "I don't ever have more money than bills!" Bills are acquired over time based on a collection of choices that we have made. We can choose to relegate our

---

12 https://hi-in.facebook.com/ChrislBurge/posts/1015427058495660

bills based on the money we have, or we can be presumptuous in wishing that we can saddle ourselves with more bills than we have money and keep our fingers crossed that we will find a way somehow to pay our bills. Trust in God also means that I believe God can satisfy my needs with the resources He has given to me and not based on the resources I am wishing or hoping to have.

The Apostle Paul, in giving counsel to his young protegee Timothy, says, "But Godliness with contentment is great gain. For we brought nothing into this world, and it is certain we can carry nothing out" (1Timothy 6:6-7). To trust God means to be godly. Trusting God means, therefore, that we are willing to be content with the resources God has given to us. The life I desire to live and the life that God has ordained for me to live might not be the same. It is therefore of extreme importance that I follow the lead of God over my life and I make decisions based on the blessings bestowed and not primarily on the blessings hoped for. Many Christian stewards find themselves in difficult financial situations because they choose to make decisions on presumed blessings as opposed to present blessings! While faith is believing also in what God can provide for us in the future, I believe it is important that we know that the things we are desiring are a part of His divine will for our lives.

Trusting God When Our Financial Resources Are Very Low

If when we accept Jesus Christ as our Lord and Savior, that means we would never again have any financial concerns, that would be awesome! Can you imagine a life like that? No stress or worry about any bills sounds like a fairy tale for most people. I don't believe in magic or fairy tales, but I do believe that living a life without being overly concerned, stressed or worried about money is possible. This is possible not because God has unlimited money and can easily make a deposit in our bank accounts every day, but because of the trusting relationship we have established with Him as our God and not just as our supplier of money. Our trust in God is in the essence of who He is, creator, redeemer and friend. What God is able to provide for us we greatly appreciate as fringe benefits from being in a relationship with Him. When the depth of our relationship with God is based on who He is and not just based on His ability to satisfy our temporal needs, I believe that God will pour an abundance of temporal blessings in our lives. Based on my own experience with God over the past two decades of marriage, where I have never had a bill placed before me that caused me stress and anxiety, here are some ways I have found that I can trust God when it comes to money:

- **Money is not the answer.** I have never had one job that paid me more than one hundred thousand dollars annually. I have worked hard, saved and invested money wisely, but realized that my financial stability was not in the amount of money I had, but in the trust I placed in God. As I trusted God in making decisions for my family and myself, I am convinced that it was following the wisdom that God provided me with that created a solid financial stability for my family and not the amount of money I had in the bank. When we trust God, He will help us to make wise decisions that will prevent us from spending money foolishly. He will also help us to spend money on things that are durable and of even greater future value.
- **Plan for the future, but always live in the present.** Planning for the future is important. We should anticipate what our expenses will be at the end of the month or year and plan accordingly. Failure to do so means

that we are living irresponsibly and recklessly. As we plan for the future it is important for us to be mindful of the decisions we are making in the present that will have a significant impact on our future obligations and responsibilities. It is important that we learn to live contentedly in the present. This does not mean that we should deny ourselves of the necessities of life, or live like we do not have the resources that we are blessed with. Living contentedly means that I am not going to live an extravagant life today to impress others, but rather I am going to live within my means. When Jesus says in Matthew 6:25 and 34 (KJV), *"...Take no thought for your life, what ye shall eat, or what ye shall drink; nor yet your body, what ye shall put on...Take therefore no thought for the tomorrow; for the tomorrow shall take thought for the things of itself..."* Jesus was emphasizing the importance of us trusting God to provide for us in the present as well as in the future. Enjoy the blessings of today! Make good use of today's opportunity! Show God that you appreciate what He has blessed you with today by using the blessings to His name, honor and glory! I have discovered that I can enjoy life to the fullest day, while still planning for the future. I have learned that I can trust God that He is able to take care of me today and in the future.

- **Don't be afraid to give.** Most, if not all, of what we do is really based on two conflicting opposites that are not able to exist in the same room at the same time: fear and faith. We can do good, real good, for ourselves, family, friends and others because of fear or faith. Hence, the motive behind what we do is sometimes more important than the thing we actually do. Doing good things because we are afraid we will not be looked at favorably by others if we don't, or that we are going to go to hell, is not a good reason for doing good. As a matter of fact, God's desire is that we do good because of faith and not fear. When the Bible counsels us to give, this is to be understood in the context of doing so based on faith and not fear. Giving is one of the counsels God has given to us to help us to overcome selfishness. Therefore, giving is not designed just to help those who are less fortunate than ourselves, but to help us become our best selves. We have discussed several Bible references about giving in previous chapters in this book because of the importance of this subject. When we are in an intimate trusting relationship with God, we will be able not only to give, but to give generously. God's desire is that we not become merely marginal Christians. That is, people who are just walking a thin line between being lost and saved. God wants us to be experiencing the abundant, generous Christian life that He has called us to experience in every area of our lives, including giving. This is what the Apostle Paul is highlighting about the Christian life when he says in Romans 8:37 (KJV), " ...*We are more than conquerors through Him who loved us.*"

- **Don't limit God.** Trusting God means that we believe that God is limitless. He can do all things and He is inexhaustible. Since this is the case, we believe that God can provide for all of our needs regardless of their magnitude or nature. Since God owns everything and He is willing to satisfy all my needs when I am in partnership and relationship with Him, I can go to God in confidence that all of my needs will be met according to His will for my life. When I do not receive something that I wanted God to provide me with, that does not mean God was not able to address that need or that I placed limitations on God. When I come to God, whom I recognize as limitless, that does not mean that I believe God is obligated to give to me everything I want or believe I need. The limitless God also has the authority to exercise His limitlessness of omniscience in determining what He decides I should receive or not. Too often we want God to show up and show off for us that He is limitless in providing the things we desire, but we do not want Him to exercise His limitless knowledge to give us what He knows is best for us. Trusting in God means that I am not going to place any limits on God's ability to provide for me or on God's knowledge to decide what He should bless me with.

God's desire is that we place our complete confidence and trust in Him and not in the things He has blessed us with. Things have limitations, but God does not. God is able to provide for us far beyond the capabilities of money. He does not want us to deny ourselves the copious measures of blessings He has in store for us, because we placed our trust in the created and not the creator.

Takeaways from Chapter 11

(The answer to the all-important question **(How do you avoid struggling financially regardless of the amount of money you have?)**

- ☐ God desires complete trust in Him for us to be the good steward He has called us to be.
- ☐ Good relationships are based on trust.
- ☐ We truly trust what and who we believe we know.
- ☐ Trusting God will result in a change of attitude toward the people and things He has asked us to be good stewards of.
- ☐ Trusting God means that I am willing to allow God to fully direct my life.
- ☐ Trusting God means taking Him at His word.
- ☐ Many Christian stewards find themselves in difficult financial situations because they choose to make decisions on presumed blessings as opposed to present blessings!
- ☐ We can trust God in all situations.
- ☐ Money does not provide us with financial stability. Trusting God does!
- ☐ Plan for the future, but live in the present.
- ☐ Don't be afraid to give!
- ☐ Do not put limitations on God!
- ☐ Trust in the creator and not in the created!

CHAPTER 12

The Big Possibilities

Enjoying Freedom in the Midst of Restriction

The promises of God are not fantasies! They are real and represent a reflection of the character of God. They are not just wishful thinking on our part to make us feel better when we are in a predicament; they are the big possibilities of hope and prosperity that God offers us when we reflect the characteristics of the good stewards that He has called us to be. The Bible is replete with big possibilities that God offers all those who are God-fearing stewards of all the resources entrusted unto them.

It may be difficult for you as you read this to imagine what life would be like with all of your needs met. All of your financial needs met, wow! All of your emotional needs are taken care of, no issues! All of your social, mental, physiological and spiritual needs are met in ways that you can only describe as awesome! This may sound too good to be true to you, but this is not fantasy or a fairy tale; there is a big possibility that you can enjoy life just like I described earlier.

God is not limited in providing for our every need. God in His omniscience may decide not to provide us with some things as we request of Him at a certain time, but that in no way means that God is not able to provide. God's greatest desire for our lives is not to give us an abundance of stuff, even though He is able to do that, but rather He is more concerned about saving us. Therefore, if God in His sovereignty decides not to give me something that I am in need of because I am not able to be a good steward of that thing and remain in an intimate relationship with Him, then I will not complain. The more I become like Jesus, the more temporal blessings God can bestow upon me and the more I remain faithful to Him. While I enjoy living with the possibility that God is able to provide me with anything I need, I take comfort in the fact that God knows what is best for me at all times. It is reassuring for us to always remember that God does not make promises that He cannot keep. Whatever He promises, He is able to provide.

We have discussed some of the promises of God in previous chapters that remind us that God delights in blessing us abundantly (Malachi 3:8-11, Luke 6:38, Acts 20:35 and 2 Corinthians 9:6-8). Some of these promises present us with such great possibilities that they cause me to wonder sometimes if most Believers really embrace them to be true. The blessings of God provide us with such big possibilities that everyone who reads and understands the Bible should be motivated to be in an intimate relationship with Jesus. There are two main categories of blessings that I would like to focus on in this chapter, which I believe give us the assurance of big possibilities that we can enjoy as good stewards of the resources God has entrusted unto us. These two categories are material blessings and financial blessings and can be found in one of my favorite Bible verses, Philippians 4:19, which says, *"But my God shall supply all your needs according to his riches in glory by Christ Jesus."* There are many biblical scholars who will emphasize the many spiritual blessings that God provides. They will underscore the point that the greatest blessings from God are the spiritual ones and that we should be more concerned about receiving the spiritual blessings over the material ones. While I believe that the spiritual blessings ought to be desired, I believe God also wants us to embrace the many material blessings He also provides for us. I believe the Bible gives us numerous examples of God pouring out in copious measures material blessings upon His people. God cares about how we live now and how we will live eternally.

Think about this verse (Philippians 4:19) carefully for a few moments, and ask yourself the following questions: Do I truly believe that God will provide for all my needs? Does this promise sound like it is too good to be true? If you were a member of the Philippian church that Paul was addressing in this letter, how would you feel, excited, happy or overwhelmed with joy? Or would you say something along the lines of, "It sounds really good, but I am not sure if God will really supply all my needs!" Let us examine the context of Paul's letter to the Philippian church and find out if this verse is truly saying what it sounds like it is saying on the surface.

The Apostle Paul is grateful to the Lord for allowing the Philippian church to continually think of him with generous hearts. He tells the church that he has learned to be content with whatever the Lord has blessed him with, for he knows what it is like to be poor and he knows what it is like to have plenty. God has given him the strength to live in any conditions. Paul thanked God for the Philippian church that has supported him financially not only when he was with them in Philippi, but also when he was preaching the gospel in Macedonia and Thessalonica. As the Apostle Paul reflected on the generosity of the church at Philippi, he was moved with heartfelt gratitude toward them. He then assures them that in the same manner that they were a blessing in addressing his financial needs, "God shall also supply all their needs according to his riches in Christ Jesus." In other words, God shall supply all the needs of those who supply the need of His work! Another way to convey the message is to say, "My God shall supply all the needs of those who partner with Him in ministry."

The Big Possibilities of Financial Blessings

Paul is here speaking specifically about the financial needs of the Philippian church. The same need he has that God used the Philippian church to address is what Paul is speaking about in this verse. God will supply all of the financial needs of those who are willing to be used by God to support the work of the proclamation of the gospel. This is an enormous possibility that we are guaranteed when we partner with God. All of our financial needs will be adequately met! Somebody might be reading this and saying right now, "Really, I will believe that when I experience it." Is there anything that God cannot do? The answer of course is a resounding No! God can do anything He desires to do, including satisfying all of my financial needs. The question we need to ask ourselves is not whether God can or will provide for our financial needs, but rather, am I able to remain in an intimate relationship with God based on loving obedience to Him, if He satisfies all of my financial needs? For many people all of our material needs are associated in some ways with our financial needs.

Therefore, our financial needs still rank as our important need. Many psychologists would argue that all needs do not have to be linked directly to finances and that there are other important needs we have that need to be addressed for our daily survival.

Russian-American psychologist Abraham Maslow in his 1943 paper proposed a theory of human motivation that is known as "Maslow's hierarchy of needs." Maslow's hierarchy of needs is a motivational theory in psychology comprising of five-tier model of human needs, often depicted as hierarchical levels within a pyramid. From the bottom of the hierarchy upwards, the needs are: physiological (food and clothing), safety (job security), love and belonging (friendship), esteem, and self-actualization. Needs lower down in the hierarchy must be satisfied before individuals can attend to needs higher up."[13]

While finances may have some influence on Maslow's hierarchy of needs, finances may not have any influence on some of the needs, especially at the top of the pyramid. However, it is important to note that God can supply all needs abundantly. Many centuries before Maslow's theory, Jesus recognized these needs and taught His disciples to ask God to provide for all their temporal needs. Jesus demonstrated the importance of satisfying the need for food when He fed over five thousand hungry people with five loaves and two fish. When it was time to pay the annual tax due to Caesar, Jesus performed a miracle to ensure that He and his disciples were not accused of not paying taxes (Matthew 17:24-27). Jesus was concerned about addressing all of the temporal needs that

---

13   https://www.simplypsychology.org/maslow.html

human beings had an obligation to address. This means that I can live with the possibility that all of my temporal needs can be satisfied by Jesus.

The important thing for us to remember as we look at Maslow's hierarchy of needs is that God can and shall supply all five levels of Maslow's hierarchy of needs and more to those who are co-laborers with Him. God's desire is for us to enjoy life on earth. While it is true that sin has marred the earth and that God will recreate the earth when Jesus returns, that does not mean that God wants us to suffer and live in abject poverty. In the model prayer Jesus taught His disciples, there is a request mentioned in the middle of that prayer: "Give us this day our daily bread." Satisfying our need for food seems to be more important to Jesus than satisfying our need for money. As important as money is to us, God is able to provide for our needs without providing us with money.

The Big Possibilities of "Stress Free Living!"

Life can become overwhelming and spiral out of control if not managed adequately. With the demands of work, school, home, church, relationships and financial obligations, the list goes on. While stress is a natural reaction by the body when certain significant changes occur that may cause emotional, mental and physical changes, it is important to have a system in place that provides the support needed to avoid severe illness and death. The pressures of life can be really demanding; however, it is possible for us to live a life of minimal stress by making and living by certain principles during the "stress-free zones" of life to cope adequately in the "stress zones."

Health Stress

Since life is not stagnant, but ever changing with each passing moment, there is always some level of stress that is always occurring. The goal in life is not necessarily to eliminate stress, but to manage the effects of the stress levels that we are faced with on a daily basis. In order for us to manage the stress levels in meaningful ways, we first must identify the things in life that we have control over and the things we do not have control over. With the things we have control over we should explore ways in which we can make decisions to reduce the stress levels that are a result of our actions. Eating a more balanced diet may reduce or eliminate the health challenges that we are experiencing. So if we have the resources that can provide us with a better diet than the one we are currently eating, we should endeavor to make the necessary changes to minimize the stress levels with our health. Our responsibility is to maximize the possibility of living a minimized life of stress. This can be achieved when we ask God to help us be the good stewards of our health and well-being that He has called us to be. Good stewardship always produces good results!

There are many occasions in life when we do not have control over the thing or person that may be the source of our stress. The coronavirus pandemic is one example of something that causes stress that we have no direct control over. By that I mean we cannot control it, stop it or eliminate it. However, we have a choice as to the way we will respond to it. We can follow the health protocols that the World Health Organization and the Centers for Disease Control and Prevention strongly recommend we follow, or we can decide to ignore all the mandates they issue. Being good stewards means managing the information we receive from others in a manner that is to our greatest benefit. We can live in a world of great stress and anxiety, yet we are experiencing low levels of stress because of the decisions we make about the information we receive.

Financial Stress

Another way we can minimize the levels of stress we are faced with every day is to make a decision to live within our means. Living within our means, means more than just making a budget. Making a budget is the first step. Living within the parameters of the budget is where the challenge comes in for many individuals. To live within a budget requires first that the budget is a realistic one that is accepted by all whom serves to govern. Once the budget has been accepted by all concerned, steps should still be made to avoid unnecessary spending even if the budget makes allowance for such spending. When we learn to be content with the material blessings God has given to us and manage them to His name, honor and glory, we will reduce the levels of financial stress significantly, and live a happy life.

Relationship Stress

I have heard the phrase "no man is an island, no man stands alone" almost all my life. The message here is not anti-singleness, anti-independence or anti-alone time, but rather that as human beings we are created to be in relationship with others. It is virtually impossible for us to live for an extended period of time without being in a relationship of some level with someone. While relationships are of extreme importance to all of us, they can also be the cause of the greatest stress we experience. This is true of all human relationships; the level of stress we experience can sometimes be astronomical! So what can we do to minimize the stress level in these most important relationships that we must have?

One of the first things I believe that can help us in our relationships is investing as much time as possible in getting to know someone before making the decision to trust and confide in that person. One of the key principles of stewardship that we have discussed earlier in this book is time. The principle of time is invaluable and is of great importance in almost all aspects of life. Oftentimes much of the stress we experience in relationships is as a result of misplaced and/or misguided trust. While there are no formulas that can provide us with the specific length of time that must be invested in a relationship before we begin to trust, we should not ignore the things we are learning about others as we interact with them in getting to know them better.

Stress in relationships is also caused by unrealistic expectations. It is important that we do not set ourselves up for failure and/or unmet desires because our expectations of others are not realistic. We must be careful not to be presumptuous to believe that what we desire from someone we can and will always receive because of the nature of our relationship. Sometimes the individual is not able to meet our expectations because he or she does not have the resources to meet them. Sometimes our expectations are more about demonstrating and exhibiting our own selfish desires than about the other person not being able to meet them. Being good stewards reminds us that God is the owner of everything, and that God will give to us that which He knows is best for us at all times. The things we at times expect from others that we do not receive may be as a result of divine intervention and not only based on human relationships.

The Big Possibilities of Eternal Life

One of the most important things being a good steward prepares us for is eternal life. This is the great possibility that all Christians are living for. Stewardship deals with the root cause of sin: selfishness. The message of the good steward is sharing how he or she has gained victory over selfishness and has allowed God to take His rightful place of preeminence in his/her heart, which has resulted in Him being first in everything the person does. This means we are willing to allow God to lead our lives in helping us to become selfless. As stewards we are asked to manage, not confiscate, the resources entrusted to us by God.

Eternal life begins now as well as later. Sounds oxymoronic, but it is true. So how can something begin now, but also begin later? According to the gospel of John 10: 27-28, Jesus says, *"My sheep hear my voice, and I know them, and they follow me: and I give unto them eternal life; and they shall never perish."* Eternal life begins when someone decides to follow Jesus. Following Jesus means being and living like Jesus. John is saying in these verses that when someone accepts the teachings of Jesus and decides to live accordingly, such an individual is now living a life that death does not have power over. This means that the good steward begins to enjoy the big possibility of eternal life even before Jesus' second coming.

Eternal life also begins later. In the gospel of Luke 13:23-24, Jesus responds to the question of eternal life this way: "Then said one unto him, Lord are there few that be saved? And He said unto them, strive to enter in at the strait gate for many I say unto you, will seek to enter in, and shall not be able." In this instance, Jesus is speaking about eternal life as a future event. Eternal life is the greatest event that a person can accomplish in the future. This means that stewards have an opportunity to become better managers of all that God offers for us in order to inherit eternal life. We can become better stewards of our time, ensuring that our priorities place the things that pertain to eternal life at the top of the list of most important things to do. We can ensure that we become good stewards of our finances and not allow poor stewardship of money to prevent us from missing out on eternal life. It is important that as stewards we maximize the time we have each day in becoming good stewards for God, so that we will be recipients of the eternal life God offers to all.

In order for us to take advantage of all the big possibilities that God has available for us, we must ensure that Jesus is with us. This means that we are in an intimate relationship with Him. It is impossible for us to take advantage of these great possibilities without divine assistance. During the 1990s the Chicago Bulls basketball team dominated the National Basketball Association. The team won six NBA championships during the same time period and was a contender for the NBA championship title every year in the 1990s. What made the team such a dominant force during that decade? The real question should be who and not what? The team consistently enjoyed the big possibility as champions every season in the 1990s because they had the greatest player in Michael Jordan, playing as their starting shooting guard. While it is true that Michael Jordan had a complement of good players as teammates around him each season, it was his positive influence on them that contributed to their high performance each game. The Chicago Bulls had a big possibility of becoming champions each year as long as Michael Jordan was on the team.

As Christian stewards of God, we too are on a team that is guaranteed a big possibility of victory each year because Michael the archangel (Jesus) is on our team. As long as we allow Jesus to lead and influence us to be the best stewards He has called us to be, the possibility is endless.

Takeaways from Chapter 12

The answer to the all-important question **(How do you avoid struggling financially regardless of the amount of money you have?)**

- ☐ The more I become like Jesus, the more temporal blessings God can bestow upon me and the more I remain faithful to Him.

- ☐ God also wants us to embrace the many material blessings that He also provides for us.

- ☐ God shall supply all the needs of those who supply the need of His work!

- ☐ My God shall supply all the needs of those who partner with Him in ministry.

- ☐ God will supply all of the financial needs of those who are willing to be used by Him to support the work of the proclamation of the gospel.

- ☐ Am I able to remain in an intimate relationship with God based on loving obedience to Him, if He satisfies all of my financial needs?

- ☐ When we learn to be content with the material blessings God has given to us and manage them to His name, honor and glory, we will reduce the levels of financial stress significantly, and live a happy life.

- ☐ Oftentimes much of the stress we experience in relationships is as a result of misplaced and/or misguided trust.

- [ ] One of the most important things that being a good steward prepares us for is eternal life.

- [ ] Stewardship deals with the root cause of sin: selfishness. The message of the good steward is sharing how he or she has gained victory over selfishness and has allowed God to take His rightful place of preeminence in his/her heart, which has resulted in Him being first in everything the person does.

You can give without loving,
but you cannot love without giving.

CHAPTER 13

The Big Stories

Testimonies of the Transforming Power of God

God Cannot Lie

My name is Daniel Archie and I am a member of the South Ozone Park Seventh-day Adventist Church, where I serve the church as an Elder and as the Stewardship director. I would like to share the blessings that God has poured out on me, not due to anything in me, but because of his faithfulness to His word.

    Several years ago, I was laid off from my job where I had previously been employed for about 27 years. I never thought it would happen to me; after all, I was hired right out of college, and most people admired the skilled work that I did. I was comfortable where I was, perhaps too comfortable. Being laid off from my job was emotionally disturbing and financially challenging. It is as if I had lost everything! Our insurance coverage only lasted for a short period of time and so did unemployment, which I was not eligible for. Along with thoughts of not finding another job, or where the money would come from to pay bills and purchase food, came, of course, the nail-biting question, "What if someone gets sick?," which became a constant worry.

I was so familiar with the promise and challenge that God gives to His people in Malachi 3:10 and 11. Yet I, and many others, habitually repeat the verse each week when tithes and offering are collected, devoid of feeling. I did not take God at His Word in faith or try to prove Him! I admit, I did worry a lot! Here is where my nail-biting test began!

- My child had an accident which required an emergency room visit. Of all the times in the world for your child to get sick, after your insurance expires. The bill for the emergency room visit was $900, not including the three doctors who did the examinations, medication and must-do procedures. "Where are we going to get the money, Lord?"
- Then one night, I broke my toe! Another emergency room visit, this time as an adult. There were X-rays, radiology, two doctors, no insurance and a $12,000 bill! "Where are we going to get the money, Lord?"
- Then there was a trip to our child's ophthalmologist three months before I was laid off, and was now presented to the insurance company to be paid. The bill was $400 for our child's examination. These were the words I heard: "Sorry, you have no insurance and you must pay the bill." Once again, "Where are we going to get the money, Lord?"
- One day God told us to call the billing center of the hospital and the eye doctor. We were going to ask them if we could pay the bill in monthly installments. To our

- amazement, both offices said, "We are going to lower your bills; please pay $40 for the hospital bill and $14 for the eye doctor and that will cover the payment for the entire bill." A $12,000 bill reduced to $54! To this day, I cannot explain how or why this happened—only God can!
- We had one car, so my wife would leave the car for me to use and walk one hour to and from her job so that I could go to interviews. I drove to a few places and the doctors who knew me tried finding part-time work for me. I was on the phone with a doctor one day and the next moment I found myself filling out an application to work in an NYC hospital. Although I no longer work in that NYC hospital, God has found me full-time employment at a hospital closer to home. To God be the glory!

I was the one who doubted God. He not only provided for my needs, but sustained my family during the time I was not working. There isn't anything too hard for God to do! He is faithful to his promises. I made a covenant with God many years ago that I would, with His help, willingly return a faithful tithe and offering. What is even more important to note is that I always have enough to pay my bills. I have never again doubted God's word in Malachi 3:10-11.

In Numbers 23:19 (KJV), the Bible says, "God is not a man that he should lie; neither the son of man that he should repent: hath he said, and shall he not do it? Or hath he spoken, and shall he not make it good?" This text assures us that we can trust God and depend on His word. He is faithful and His mercies are new every morning!

In the book *Ministry of Healing*, in the chapter entitled "A Higher Experience," you will find these words to strengthen your faith: "He (God) is well pleased when we urge past mercies and blessings as a reason why He should bestow on us greater blessings. He will more than fulfill the expectations of those who trust fully in Him." When I reflect on how God provided for my family, I could only trust Him to see me through and provide the best for me regarding employment. I am happy to say that He opened the windows of Heaven and poured out blessings and my cup is overflowing. God is true to His word. He is the true and living God that cannot lie. All we need to do is trust, obey and faithfully return our first fruits to Him. Continue to be faithful stewards to God so that His name may be glorified through you.

– Daniel

Overcoming Hurdles: Challenges and Changes

When I was asked to write this testimonial, I did not know where to begin. Admittedly, I was not always a good steward of money and time. I, like so many, had little understanding of both. I wasted both on events that had no futuristic rewards.

My change came in 1976 when I accepted the Advent message. From the beginning, the Sabbath and tithing were my biggest hurdles. It was difficult at first, but I welcomed the challenge and change in my life because I wanted something different that would give my life purpose and meaning. The first time I gave 10% of my income as tithe, I was in shock. I believe that I nearly had a heart attack. This was much different from the usual $5 I would normally put in the offering plate. In addition, my mother was taking 60% of my income.

Nevertheless, I pledged to give willingly and faithfully to the Lord.

The following year I applied to only one college and was accepted. The first semester was extremely challenging, I was not given a room in the dormitory and had to find alternative housing at the YWCA. However, God had things under control; a lovely non-Seventh-day-Adventist family took me to live in their home at no charge. They treated me, a perfect stranger, as a part of their family with love and compassion. From the beginning of the second semester to the time of my graduation three years later, I was blessed with a tuition scholarship. I was able to graduate with honors and had very few loans to repay.

By God's grace, I continued to return tithes and offerings from all the summer jobs that God provided me with. I applied to seven medical schools and was blessed to be accepted to the school of my first choice. My excitement was short-lived, because I had no money for tuition. Once again, I decided to trust in God to make a way out for me and He did. I was blessed with another tuition scholarship for the four years I was in medical school. When it was time to graduate, I only had a small student loan debt to repay. Since God was so faithful to me, I pledged to be faithful to Him. I had a challenge with the schedule of my anatomy class that met on Sabbaths. However, I decided to honor God by going to church on Sabbaths and not to my class. The Lord helped me to pass all my classes and I met some of my dearest friends in church at the Emmanuel Temple Seventh-day Adventist Church in Buffalo, New York. The Lord continued to bless me through my residency and fellowship programs, and I continued to be faithful to Him with my tithe and offering.

I was blessed with the opportunity after my years in school to take care of my beloved mother. When my mother returned to church with me, I noticed that she was also returning a faithful tithe and offerings to the Lord. God later blessed her with her own home and she continued to be faithful to God in returning tithe and offerings. God's blessing on me has continued over the years since 1976. I am blessed with a husband of 26 years and counting, two adult children, and a beautiful home. "God loves a cheerful giver!" By God's grace, I believe I am one.

– Donna

The Struggle Was Real!

Many years ago, as I passed through the early portion of the third decade of my life, I contemplated the concept of returning a tithe. I took the simple position that, as an act of worship, no one would be allowed to dictate to me the terms by which my tithe would be returned. How much to return, on what income, or how frequently. In my mind, it was based on 10% of net income. Thus it was a private and personal matter. Net income was defined as the money left in my care after the government had taken its portion, as well as what is remaining after all expenses are paid from other enterprises. My offering naturally would be based on how blessed I had become or on what I determined to be a blessing. I also speculated that tithing was more probably a method of extracting more money from already poor third-world church members, using indoctrinated clergy to perpetuate social and economic control by white Anglo-Saxons and Europeans, perhaps using the Bible and church organization as a crutch.

I was, at best, a skeptical and marginal tithe-returning member of the Seventh-day Adventist church. Somewhere during the fourth decade of my life, our church was being ministered to by a senior pastor of good experience and reasonable humility. I cannot recollect what occasioned him to present a sermon on good stewardship. It is, however, safe to say that it was during a time when the church was in financial malnutrition as a result of the poor commitment to the financial support of the institution by its members.

His presentation was interesting and gripping. I listened intently, all the while paying attention to those details that justified his beliefs in good stewardship. On occasion, I scribbled down a few keys and interesting scriptural references. My intent was to make a thorough review of those texts in the quietness of my home. It was my view to underscore those innuendos and weaknesses in the preacher's line of discussion. Furthermore, I would use the discovered weaknesses to solidify or destroy my concept of good stewardship and, in particular, to come to a final and reliable resting place as to what, how, and when my tithe should be returned.

On reviewing the blessing that Abraham received, on giving to Melchizedek, king of Salem (priest of the most-high God) 10% of the spoils of war, for granting him victory (Gen: 14) over King Chedorlaomer and his mighty host, it became clear to me that blessings are in store for those who try to have and indeed do have a covenant and worship relationship with Melchizedek (priest of the most-high God). As of that time, I have been returning a faithful tithe on my gross income and an offering to show my thanks. This act of worship has now become a source of many blessings.

(Anonymous)

How Papa Changed My Attitude Toward Returning Tithe

I grew up with both parents in Jamaica, West Indies. When we were children, my father started us off by returning tithe and offering long before we were even baptized. So, long before I had a job, I returned a tithe from any monetary gifts I received.

When I became an adult, I continued to return a tithe. I got married and had a son. Things in my life changed drastically because of the high cost of living. Things were very expensive, and taking care of a young baby was extremely difficult. My husband was not accustomed to returning a tithe, so when he saw me doing so, he thought that I was giving away hard-earned money for no reason. Eventually, I stopped returning tithe and giving offerings altogether. Since my husband was never a returner of tithe and giving offerings, we spent everything we earned. However, we found ourselves always in need of help during the month. I started visiting my father in the country to borrow money from him regularly to meet our monthly expenses. He never questioned me about the frequency of my borrowing; he just kept on loaning to me even though oftentimes I was not able to repay him.

One Sunday, when I went to the country for my regular visit and to borrow more money, my father said to me, "Girl, are you returning tithe?" I told him we could not afford to do that because we were raising a family. He proceeded to give me a lecture about what the Bible said about people who rob God. He said, "You call yourself working as a teacher and your husband working for the government, and yet you come to borrow money from me as a farmer. You need to trust God and return His tithe first before you do anything, and I guarantee you that your money problem will be over." Then he went on to remind me that his farm was able to feed and clothe five children and that we were never in need of important things.

From that day, I never asked my father to lend me any money, and I was always able to return a faithful tithe, give an offering, pay my bills, and even have excess money to save each month. God keeps His promises! Go ahead and step out in faith and see what God will do for you when you put Him first in your life.

(Anonymous)

How a Tenant Restored My Faithfulness to God

Before I bought my house, I returned a faithful tithe. My salary was great, and returning a tithe was not a problem. I returned a faithful tithe and offering for several years. After buying a house, I faced large monthly bills, and so I figured that the Lord understood my problems. I did not think I could return my tithe anymore, so I only gave a little offering. I knew that I was not doing what God expected from me, but I thought I just could not do any better.

With mounting bills every month, I decided to rent out a part of the house. I rented out the first floor and decided to use the rent to return the tithe I should be giving from the income from my job. Then it occurred to me that with the additional income from the rent I was receiving, I also had to return a tithe. While the tenant paid her rent, I would return some of the money as a little tithe, but I still knew that that was not enough. Then one day, my tenant stopped paying her rent! This created a terrible financial problem for me.

I listened to a sermon and was convicted by the Spirit that I should honor God with tithe and offerings. I made up my mind by the grace of God to return an honest tithe to the Lord. I told the Lord that if the tenant started paying her rent regularly again, I would return a tithe on both my salary and the rent. God moved upon the heart of my tenant, and in a matter of days, she brought the rent in arrears and started regularly paying again. I was amazed at the way God intervened on my behalf. From that day, I thank God for working through my tenant to restore my faithfulness to Him. To God be the glory!

(Anonymous)

When Will God Provide?

When I was growing up, my parents always taught me that God provides. As a child, one of the hardest lessons I had to learn after working so hard for the money I received for the job I did is that I now had to return 10% tithe to God, as well as give a love offering to show my appreciation to God for what He has done for me.

My parents told me, "Son, one day, you will realize that giving back to God is the best thing you can do!" Well, I guess one day came sooner than I thought. It was while I was still trying to discover life during my teenage years when I received a call from my father from a hospital bed. Dad shared with me that the other vehicle ran the stop sign and hit the vehicle my dad and his coworker were traveling in. The force of the impact caused the van they were traveling in to flip over three times. Due to the accident, my father sustained a bulging disc and pinched nerves. As a bricklayer, this meant he would be out of work for an extended period of time. During this time, my mother was in college studying to be a nurse. This meant that for several weeks or months, there was going to be absolutely no income coming to our home. Soon the bills began piling up, and the food we usually had in the refrigerator and cupboards became lesser and lesser. I can remember as a teenager wondering, "When is God going to start providing for us in this situation? When will He come through for my family in our desperate situation?"

One day my parents, as their custom, called for us to have evening worship. As soon as our worship time ended, the doorbell rang. Standing at the door was my aunt. She said she happened to be at the market, and something told her to pass by our house. When she came inside, she was carrying a big box load of chicken and other groceries. It was then that my father shared with his sister about our current financial hardship and that she was an answer to our prayers. God used her to provide for us when we never expected it.

Never had I witnessed a miracle like that before. We had just finished praying at the end of our evening worship, and as soon as we said amen, God was right at our front door with the answer to our prayer. God provided immediately! This miracle helped me as I grew in Christ. I became confident from that moment that God was indeed a great provider for His children.

– Neville

"Paying" an Honest Tithe and Giving a Liberal Offering

Recently I lost my job. After not working for more than two months, the bills began to pile up. During this time, to make matters worse, my car and my son's car broke down. There was absolutely no money for car repairs at this time. I got up each morning with sometimes faith and sometimes fear, not knowing if or when I would get a job. However, I never lost hope. I continued praying and trusting God for a job.

One morning after rising from my knees, I checked my email and noticed that I was invited for an interview from one of the several places that I had applied for a job. On the day of the interview, I asked God for direction and promised Him that I would continue to be faithful in returning tithe and offerings if I got the job. A few weeks later, I was offered a job. However, unfortunately, I had to work for two months before getting my first paycheck. Without public transportation available to me, I rented a car. This, of course, caused me to increase my debt. I had to increase my financial burden, but at least I was mobile.

When I received my first paycheck, I knew that my first obligation was to "pay" my tithe and give a liberal offering. However, I struggled with the idea of buying a car first before returning my tithe and offering. During the time of the offertory, I was still struggling with making the right decision. The Spirit appealed to me, and I wrote the check for the full amount of tithe and gave a liberal offering. I whispered to myself, "I am going to trust God!" A few days later, I received a check that I was not expecting. I returned my tithe and offering from it, paid for the rental car I was driving, paid off some other bills, and bought myself a car. I am so glad I trusted God to do the right thing. God is truly amazing! I am truly convinced that when we return an honest tithe and give a liberal offering, adversities can be turned into blessings!

– Heather

Trusting God When It Doesn't Make Sense

After spending a considerable amount of time in preparation for this sacred and special ceremony, I was baptized in 1971 by Pastor Etzer Obas. During my preparation for baptism, Pastor Obas taught me the importance of being systematically faithful to God when it comes to my finances. By the grace of God, I have maintained the principles he taught me throughout my life from that time forward. Since putting these tools into practice, my life has been fortified. Not wanting to keep these blessings to myself, I have shared my experience with several others. I have had the pleasure to see friends and parishioners that I have advised testifying about the results of trusting God with their finances. This gives me a rich panoply of experiences and testimonies that I could share with the readers of this book. I will share one of my experiences when I was called to wage war in ministry in North America. This began in the cool town of Rochester, New York.

From 1998-2001, I was lovingly helping the El-Siloe Seventh-day Adventist Church in Lynn, Massachusetts. In November of 2001, I received the call to minister as the pastor of the then Rocher des Siecles Seventh-day Adventist Mission, which has since become the Capernaum Seventh-day Adventist Church. At the time of my assignment by the Northeastern Conference of Seventh-day Adventists to minister in Rochester, I was employed secularly by the Town of Randolph,

Massachusetts, as an ESL Haitian Community Liaison. My wife was working for a private dental office in Medford, Massachusetts. During this time, money relatively blossomed in our pockets every Thursday. But, just as Peter abandoned his nets to follow Christ, my family and I left everything behind in Massachusetts and responded to the Lord's call in Rochester, New York.

The Thursdays that we used to look forward to and enjoy quickly became different. Money became extremely tight! My wife had given up her job in Medford, MA, and was unemployed in Rochester, NY. Although she was unceasingly looking for job opportunities, all the interviews ended with a refusal to allow her to keep the Sabbath holy. Therefore, we were constrained to live on one salary. I was not only earning less than I was paid in Randolph, MA but I was not getting paid every Thursday as I did before.

Nevertheless, twice per month, my commitment of 15% (tithe 10% and offering 5%) of our single income was faithfully remitted to the church of God. We quickly had to become strategic with our budgeting. After covering one or two bills and buying some meager groceries for two adults and three children, a full gallon of milk became a luxury. It was exactly during this time that my wife and I made the decision to test our faith and give God a greater percentage of our single income. We went from 15% to 20% (10% tithe and 10% offering). Foolish! Right? No, wrong! The first weekend that I gave the check, my wife was offered a job the following Monday to Friday, with flexible hours on Fridays according to the season of the year. Extraordinary, isn't it? Our test of faith yielded as God promised!

Habakkuk 2:4 (KJV) says, "The just shall live by faith." We believed and proved Him in faith, and He provided! My wife was able to keep this employment until my new assignment to

Brooklyn almost a decade later. She is still pursuing her dental career, and I am still ministering in the church of the Lord.

In the Review and Herald, September 18, 1888, Ellen G. White says, "He has linked us to Himself by all these tokens in heaven and on earth. He watches over us with more tenderness than does a mother over an afflicted child."

– Othnel

I Believe I'll Testify – The Blessings I Received from Giving Cheerfully

My personal "faith bucket challenge" of returning 10% tithe and 10% offering started over 15 years ago. It began one day when I listened to a sermon where the preacher quoted the Bible verse that says, "The same measure that we give, the Lord gives to us!" (Luke 6:38).

I was always faithful in returning the tithe but giving little or no offering. One day I heard a presentation by two brothers from my church, and I had a radical change in perspective about my giving pattern to God. They were encouraging the church to give, as usual, 10% of their gross income as tithe and 5% as an offering. Initially, I said to myself that a total of 15% sounds like a whole lot to give. However, I decided that I would start to do just what they were recommending. As soon as I started to return the 15% in total (tithe and offering) against my gross income, I saw almost immediately multiple blessings from the Lord pouring into my life. My income increased, and my family life just got better. I concluded that if God blessed me so abundantly for giving 15%, I believe He will bless me even more if I return 20% (10% tithe and 10% offering).

So with confidence, I started giving 20% in total back to God. The Lord, in return, blessed me with a copious measure of financial blessings. He provided me with great employment opportunities that gave me the flexibility to work and spend time addressing the cares and needs of my kids. The income from work was the best I had ever received. I left one job and went to another that paid lower than the previous one, but I saw the hand of God providing for my family and me. I was able to send my children to Seventh-day Adventist institutions from elementary school through universities. All four of my children are Oakwood University graduates. My children's tuition and other bills may be staring me in the face, but God always comes through and takes care of it. I am confident that God will continue to take care of my family.

My faith in God grew so much through the faithful returning of tithe and offering. As a result, I feel extremely confident when I pray for other areas of my life, such as the sick and suffering. I have even changed my approach to praying: I spend more time thanking God for all of His goodness and mercies towards my family and me before making any request of Him. I have proven that God keeps His promises and covenants with us. If we keep our side of the promises and covenants, we will experience God's blessings (financial) and otherwise in our lives.

(Anonymous)

I Took the Challenge: Leading by Example

When we, as stewardship directors, were asked to promote the "Faith Bucket Challenge" (10% tithe and 10% offering) in our churches, I knew that before I could promote this campaign with sincerity, I had to be convicted by the Holy Spirit to believe the concept myself. For those who do not know, the Faith Bucket Challenge is a commitment of 10 people in your church to give a faithful tithe of 10% and a generous offering of 10% for one quarter out of the year. I was already a faithful tithe payer (of the gross) and gave a somewhat liberal offering, but I had never before demonstrated a 10-10 faith. God had already proven Himself with what I was currently giving. Can you imagine what He will do if I am even more generous? I thought. Therefore, I planned my giving for one quarter before I took the challenge.

God wants us to be wise stewards of our treasure; therefore, I paid off a couple of bills and began to spend more frugally so that I could make way for more giving. I began to see how this challenge was instilling frugality in me already. It helped me develop discipline in my spending. I could see the blessings of God even before the quarter began. I got excited and could not wait for the quarter to begin. The feeling reminded me of the way my daughter acted when giving a birthday gift to a friend. My daughter would be so excited about giving that one would have thought the gift was her own. This is exactly how I felt about giving more.

Now that I was totally sold on the concept of the Faith Bucket Challenge, I began to promote it to the church body. Needless to say, when the quarter came for me to take the leap of faith, I was filled with excitement as I filled out my tithe envelope. I gave to auxiliaries that I had not given to before. When the treasurer's report was shared at the end of the month, I was happy to see the increase that the church had in the combined budget. It was an amazing feeling! I understood what it meant by the verse that I have heard for so long, "God loves a cheerful giver" (2 Corinthians 9:7).

In addition, God "rebuked the devourer for my sake" (Malachi 3:11). My 15-year-old car continues to run smoothly (after it warms up). The problem that caused the engine service light to greet me on my dashboard every time I sat behind the steering wheel was fixed. The Lord blessed my health, and I began making and eating delicious vegan dishes. God continues to open up the windows of heaven and pour me out copious measures of blessings. God keeps His word! We just need to trust Him and take Him at His word. We deny ourselves an abundance of blessings when we do not live by the word of God.

– Betsy

A Strange Conversation

I have read this text several times, and I believe that you also have. It is the well-known Bible verse found in Proverbs 3:5-6, which says, *"Trust in the Lord with all thine heart; and lean not unto thine own understanding. In all thy ways acknowledge Him, and He shall direct thy paths."* God Himself taught me the true meaning of this Bible verse. Before I share with you the details of this experience, please allow me to share with you some details of who I am to add some context to what I am about to share with you. I serve as an elder, stewardship leader, treasurer, and the HUD Area Leaders for the Elders Council.

God taught me this lesson of trust in Him while I was sitting in a pew in church during the offertory when I was a young mother. I was recently divorced, in debt, very low on money, and was trying to raise two small boys. As the deacons were making their way around the church to collect the tithes and offerings for the day, God had a full conversation with me when I declared to Him that I had nothing to give. I mean, of course, God understood my situation, right? He asked me if He had been good to me, and if so, I should be faithful in my tithes and offerings. He gave me a dollar amount and told me to write the check. I told Him that if I did that, all the checks that I wrote previously would bounce because of insufficient funds in my account.

I must be honest and tell you that after much resistance and much attitude, I agreed to write the check. I said to God, whatever happened next week was on Him! Well, God did not wait until next week to remind me about who He is. That afternoon when I got home from church, my son went into my closet to play a game. He soon came out of the closet with a wad of money that I am positive was not there before! Interestingly enough, the amount of money found by my son was the exact amount that God told me to write on the check earlier in church that same day.

On that Sabbath, God showed me that He loves me and that He will take care of me. He reminded me that He is with me and that I do not have to do it alone. I recognized that I have to be faithful to Him because He is always faithful to me.

– Viveen

God's Blessings Are Spiritual and Material

A friend of mine reported that he was once asked to speak to a group of wealthy entrepreneurs. He reported that he spoke for about 15-20 minutes, underscoring the point several times that God's desire is to bless us spiritually and not materially. At the end of his presentation, a mutual friend of ours stayed back to speak with him for a few minutes. With both hands on his shoulders, the friend whispered in his ears, "Don't make that mistake again; come down to my office tomorrow; I have something I would like to share with you."

The next day he went down to see his friend at his office. Every square foot of the office was elegantly decorated. The boardroom, bathroom, and kitchenette were nicely furnished with high-quality furniture. His private office was warm and inviting, with a beautiful mahogany desk, customized chairs, and sofas. He reported that everything was so breathtaking he could hardly believe that it was the same space he had been into on several occasions before. After the tour of the office, he asked his friend when the transformation was done. He was told only a month ago.

The host, an attorney by profession, shared that when he started giving more to God, he started receiving more from God. "I am no longer giving God only 10% of my income; I give Him 50%. The office was run-down and looked really shabby. I decided that this was not representative of a place where a Believer in God works. So I decided that I was going to honor God with my tithe and offering and see what He would do. I made no demands on God for material blessings; I did not want to trade with God because I knew that I did not have anything of my own to trade with. So in loving obedience to God and a desire to see God's presence be manifested in our church in tangible ways, I decided to give more in the offering than I returned in tithe. The result is what you are seeing in this office."

So, once again, with both hands on his shoulders, he was reminded not to make the mistake of telling anyone that God is not interested in giving His people material blessings.

– Anonymous

Who Is Your Boss?

"The Lord is my helper, and I will not fear what man shall do unto me" (Hebrews 13:6).

Since I was 14 years old, the doors of employment have effortlessly opened for me. Does this sound boastful? Quite the contrary, I am beyond humbled by the opportunities and grateful for every door the Lord has allowed me to walk through. It would never have happened without His consent and guidance.

Like most God-fearing Christians, I believe that God is the sole owner of everything within ourselves and our world (Psalm 24:1). While at church, we hear the phrase "God is in control" quite often. We repeat the phrase to ourselves and others as if it were a mantra when we feel powerless and particularly helpless. But I often wonder whether we truly understand what that phrase means. Do our actions support that we believe He is definitely in control?

There was a time when I enjoyed working as an independent contractor. It provided me with the freedom to set my own hours and earn a high income. However, circumstances in my life quickly changed, and I had to consider a more predictable and traditional form of employment.

After researching my preferred industry, I became interested in an organization that closely matched my skills and offered a progressive environment. The challenge was to figure out how to get my foot in the door. I had no career connections within an industry that thrives on networking. Despite feeling somewhat intimidated, I chose to follow the advice of both my earthly and heavenly fathers and boldly pursued what I wanted (Joshua 1:9). Ignoring my fears, I prayed and cold-contacted the leader of the organization via email. I enclosed a persuasive well-thought-out cover letter along with my resume and waited for a response. That same afternoon, I got a response asking for an interview for the following day.

The interview went exceedingly well. I felt God's favor working through my prospective boss and me. Within six weeks, I began working at my fabulous new job. I was excited, optimistic, and above all, grateful for this new venture. Unfortunately, three weeks into the job, my joy quickly turned into pain. Although I worked diligently, I had not yet mastered the culture and expectations of my current employment. My boss was not satisfied with my performance and scrupulously questioned whether I deserved to be there. Her sudden lack of support for me made me feel insecure and worthless. Instead of recognizing a fickle and unfair moment on her part, I wondered if her judgment of me was correct. For a brief moment, I felt that my boss had absolute power over determining whether I was worthy of the position I was given.

Immediately I began to question God. Why would He allow this to happen to me? He was the one who led me to this job in the first place. What was He thinking? Before starting my job, I had asked the Lord for guidance on my job hunt. I felt His presence throughout the entire experience. He responded by granting my preference and location. He allowed me to walk into a career without the personal connections people usually depend on for that industry. He was my sole connection to my newfound job. Why on earth would He want me to leave it now?

It's at times like these that we tend to forget that God truly is in control. Instead of turning to God for empowerment and direction, we turn away from Him. We make our bosses become "Goliaths" and Godlike, believing they yield unequivocal power over us. We yield and allow them to determine our work status and any related future endeavors. We surrender our will and faith to mere mortals who are just as weak and vulnerable as we are (James 4:14). We suddenly forget our spiritual alignment and who actually sustains our lives.

Suddenly God snapped me out of my depressive stupor and reminded me it was He who provided the job that was given to me. I then understood that my boss was merely a supporting actor, not a protagonist used to execute His purpose. He showed me He was in control and had absolute power. I finally understood He would be the one to determine when my position would come to an end. Consequently, I stopped caring about my boss' musings. Instead, I prayed for His guidance (Psalm 32:8) and for excellence in my work. Thankfully, he has continued to lead me in successful outcomes for the past 13 years (and counting) since that incident.

God is our original provider and our ultimate boss. No one has power over us (Hebrews 13:6). Take the time to let that sink in. Release your insecurities and embrace the peace He is so willing to give us. Claim your new job security in the Lord. Work fearlessly and ensure that all your efforts please and honor Him (1 Corinthians 10:31). It won't guarantee that you will be void of leaders who think they can control your livelihood, but it will cause you to always remember who you actually work for.

– Daisy

What Appears Impossible Is Possible

I had an old car that was not performing mechanically or economically well, so I investigated buying a new car. The lowest-priced new car looked like an impossibility for me to afford. I concluded that based on my finances, it would be a real struggle to make the monthly payments for any car. I explored all possibilities and counted the cost. Finally, after checking out the cost to insure the car I made the decision to purchase the car.

A few days after purchasing my new car, I got the insurance policy with the detailed price outlined. As I looked over it, I realized almost immediately that the insurance quote was inaccurate. The price was far more than the insurance agent quoted to me initially. I went to the insurance agent to inform him of a mistake in the billing price. However, to my surprise when I spoke with him, he responded in a manner like that of a dragon. He told me that was the best price that I could get for the insurance coverage that I needed. I then immediately told him to cancel the insurance. He responded with more rage like a dragon again and said, "You can go to State Farm or Allstate, and you will not get a better price!"

I took his suggestion and went to the Allstate Insurance office and was quoted a price much lower than the dragon-like insurance agent quoted to me. I went next to the State Farm Insurance office and got even a much lower price quote than the one I got from Allstate. I decided to cancel the policy I had signed with Allstate a few hours before and signed up with State Farm that same day.

I was convinced that God led me in my decision and guided me to get the most affordable insurance rate using the dragon-like agent. God sometimes shows up through unlikely people and situations. My day would get even better, unbeknownst to me. I got an unexpected blessing from God that caused me to praise Him instantly. Someone, without me asking or discussing anything about the car with them, assisted me in making a monthly payment. Just when I thought God was through blessing me that day, the person decided not just to assist me with one month's payment but several consecutive months of car payments. To God be the glory!

God can make what seems impossible to you and me possible!

– Litchfield

Lessons from Observing a Squirrel

On July 6, 2017, the weather around Battery Park, New York City, was perfect for outdoor activities. While basking in the sun at the park, I spotted a squirrel roaming in my vicinity. Soon he was on my table, standing at a cross end from me. He looked me pitifully in the eyes, raising and stretching his front legs as if he was asking me for some of my muffins. I really did not mind sharing with the little creature, but my fear of animals and that this squirrel might gravitate toward me drove me to slam on the table forcefully in order to scare him away. He jumped off the table and ran and hid underneath. For fear that he might climb on my legs, I walked away to finish eating my muffin. I looked back to ensure that he was not following me, and I saw him eating crumbs that fell from the table.

After eating, I placed the wrap into a paper bag and dumped it in the bin a few feet from the table where I initially sat. I then moved to another table and witnessed a jaw-dropping scene. The squirrel went into the garbage bin and then jumped out with the paper bag that I dumped. He pulled out the muffin wrap and quickly devoured what was left. As I pondered the scenario, my thoughts drifted to the various times that I allowed fear to hinder me from giving.

My refusal to give to the squirrel did not hinder him from having his share of the muffin. Actually, he did not miss out on anything (he got what he wanted), but I missed out on an opportunity to share and to overcome my fear of a harmless creature. Fear and busyness have hindered my giving on numerous occasions. I have passed beggars on the street with money in my wallet, but too busy to stop. I have also refused to give to a person because I feared that it might become a habit. However, the episode of the squirrel reminded me that it is not always going to be safe or convenient to give. Giving has to be intentional and often requires a step of faith. Too often, I forget this well-known Bible verse: "It is more blessed to give than to receive" (Acts 20:35). Why should I neglect a blessed opportunity?

On Sabbath, August 5, 2017, I was impressed to give $20 to someone, but I only had $5.80 in my checking account. My next payday was ten days away. I borrowed the $20 I needed from my mom and promised to return it in the upcoming week before I expected to get paid. I was not sure how I would reimburse my mom so quickly, but because God impressed me to give, I decided to give even though it wasn't "safe." I was just trusting God to provide. On Thursday evening (5 days later), I assisted a young lady with some business transactions, and she gave me $100. After putting aside $10 for my tithe and $10 for my offering, I returned the $20 to my mom and gave some money to someone else as well.

– Tracy

Taking Care of His Business

I didn't even know it had a name when this "thing" entered my mind. No one called it energy conservation. At most, parents wanted to keep the light bill as low as possible, so they shouted into an empty room, "Who left the light on?" or "Shut the door. Are you cooling off the whole block?" It was embedded in my mind that I turn off the lights in other people's homes to this day!

Years later, I had an epiphany: why not work in the environmental field? Although it took a while, I turned my career toward what God put in my heart. Its name was environmental advocacy. It is actually a branch of stewardship, and not enough of us Seventh-day Adventists are talking about it.

There are numerous Bible verses in the Old and New Testaments that admonish us to care for the earth. Nature is second to the Scriptures in demonstrating undeniable evidence of God's eternal power and divine nature, so all people are without excuse for not knowing Him (Romans 1:19-20). Also, I read the lyrics of hymn 641, "God in His Love for Us," which talks about environmental stewardship. It is our moral obligation, like returning tithe and caring for the poor, in appreciation of the ultimate sacrifice of Jesus Christ for our opportunity for salvation if we choose to take advantage of it.

It is really humbling to discover our special task and then have the courage to go out and do it. Everyone has a distinct calling to do something. Over the years, creation care became my own personal mission when talking about environmental stewardship. Yours may be something else, but as God's chosen people, we must take the best care of our environment while we wait for Jesus to take us to His pristine heaven.

– Natalie

An Amazing Discovery!

I am discovering that I have many gifts. All along, I thought my gift was being financially savvy and potentially gifted in the area of teaching. I never wanted to be an actual teacher, so I ended up in the profession of a financial advisor. This profession has been a tremendous blessing, and I have learned so much about work, life, and myself.

But the thing that surprises me the most is a gift I only discovered a few years ago. God asked me to start writing and sharing, and I reluctantly said yes, after coming up with many excuses. Some of my excuses were that I was so private, who would want to listen to me anyway, and more importantly—I am not a writer. But God answered all my excuses and showed me He still had an assignment for me.

It has been over two years now, and I still marvel at the wisdom of God. I am blessed to have written two books, several blogs, vlogs, and articles for various publications. He is using me to share simple messages of His goodness. One person recently shared with me that she loved the fact that I include personal testimonies of the goodness of God without making it seem that God's plans are far-fetched from reality. Honestly, I love that too. It has taught me to open my eyes and look for what God is doing in my daily life.

In order to share with others, I have had to learn certain things that only God can teach. I am learning that stewardship is not just about finances; it is about how we manage everything that we have been assigned to do. For me, stewardship has been sharing messages of hope. I believe that if God can bring me through any situation, He can bring others through as well. He is a redeeming God! Most of all, I am able to share messages of God's love by using the gift He has given me and, at the same time, following His command of sharing the gospel with others. Luke 16:10a (ESV) states, "One who is faithful in a very little thing is also faithful in much."

Let us show ourselves faithful with whatever God has given to us so that He can entrust us with more. Continue to be faithful stewards of the resources God has given to you. If you are not sure what your talents or gifts are, ask God to reveal them to you.

– Kaysian

Bibliography

Barclay, William. Ethics in a Permissive Society (New York: Harper and Row, 1971), p. 162.

Covey, R. Stephen, Merrill, A. Roger and Merrill, Rebecca R. First Things First (New York: NY, Simon and Schuster,1994), p. 17.

Kushner, Harold K. Conquering Fear: Living Boldly in an Uncertain World (New York: Random House, Inc., 2009), p. 3.

Ryrie, Charles Caldwell Th.D., Ph.D. Ryrie Study Bible: Expanded Edition (Chicago: Moody Press, 1994), p. 985.

Strait, C. Neil. Stewardship Is More Than Time, Talent and Things (Kansas City: Beacon Hill Press, 1993), p. 3.

Swindoll, Charles R. Living Beyond the Daily Grind II (Carmel, New York: Guideposts, 1988), p. 276.

https://www.sermonillustrator.org/illustrator/sermon1a/preacher.htm

https://hi-in.facebook.com/ChrislBurge/posts/1015427058495660

https://www.datainsighttraining.com/blog/a-lesson-from-a-very-wise-man

https://www.challies.com/christian-living/7-things-your-church-needs-from-you/

https://matthewzcapps.com/2014/03/31/charles-spurgeons-the-carrot-and-the-horse/

https://www.simplypsychology.org/maslow.htmlhttps://www.worldometers.info/coronavirus/coronavirus-death-toll/

https://ministry127.com/resources/illustration/a-bad-dream

About the Author

Dr. Ferron Fitzroy Francis has been a pastor for over 20 years. He has served the church as a financial advisor/educator for his entire ministry. He has served the Northeastern Conference of Seventh-day Adventists as Financial Stewardship Director, Planned Giving and Trust Services Director, Internal Auditor, and Assistant Treasurer. He has written several scholarly articles on financial management and is the founding editor of the *Good Steward* newsletter. He has been married for over 21 years to his beautiful wife Tosha-Lyn, and they have two young-adult children, Andrew and. Ashley-Ann. Dr. Francis has a BA degree in Theology from Oakwood University, a M.A. degree in Religion from Andrews University, and a DMin degree from Hebrew Union College-Jewish Institute of Religion. He is pursuing an MBA degree in Leadership and Finance at Post University.